PANORAMAS

of the Canadian Rockies

photography by M. Buschert

essays by Robert W. Sandford

A Summerthought Publication

Banff, Alberta

Copyright © 1987 by Summerthought Ltd.

ISBN 0-919934-17-X

Editor and Graphic Designer: Thomas Owen

Colour Separations: United Graphic Services Ltd.

Printed and bound in Canada

Published by
Summerthought Ltd.
P.O. Box 1420
Banff, Alberta T0L 0C0
Canada

CONTENTS

THE PANORAMA

RESTORING VISTA TO MOUNTAINS

In returning from the Rockies, visitors are often disappointed with their pictures. The images do not represent accurately the overwhelming scale of the peaks. The mountains have little immediacy, they lack presence. They seem mere tiles culled from a grander mosaic that has to be felt as much as seen in real life. Small prints, then, are too often inexact copies of the bold experience of the mountains. It is not an easy problem to solve.

In most mountain photography there is an absence of vista. This is true even in the work of professionals. Mountains are removed from context, edited out of the vast ranges of which they are usually part. Perspective vanishes as the camera shrinks landscapes to fit the piecework reality of the viewfinder. Resulting images do not satisfy memory. They do not accurately portray the mood and huge presence of alpine scenes.

Early Panoramic Experiment

The first experiments in panorama photography were undertaken, not to give a more accurate perspective of mountains, but to create a visual sensation of flying. Early panoramas were pieced together from photographs taken from hot air balloons, and were highly salable among those who could not afford to fly themselves. The images were popular because they put the cities, where these people lived, into perspective in relation to the surrounding countryside. Now that flight is a common part of most cultures, we have a good sense of where we are in relation to the rest of our world. Panoramas are now used for other applications. Far more commonly employed in Europe where this technology has advanced most, the panorama camera has myriad applications in industry and advertising. It is also used for surveillance in large crowds. The high resolution of the panorama lens makes it possible to focus on objects very near the camera, all the way to infinity with one aperture. It is also, however, a complicated device to use.

The first panoramas were developed by combining single images. The shortcomings of this approach became obvious when photographers tried to match the seams of sequential photographs. Often the images were not constructed around the focal point of the camera and distortion occurred. Exposures were difficult to calculate and lighting had to be even throughout the scene to take full advantage of the narrow exposure latitudes of the film. For this reason, panoramas remained, and still remain, a domain of the specialist.

The new optical technology of the late twentieth century has made possible large format cameras with rotating lenses capable of encompassing 360 degrees. In these very sophisticated and expensive cameras, the lens migrates over the course of a predetermined arc while the film is transported over the focal plane. The camera that was used to make the photographs in this book utilized a 75mm normal lens instead of a wide-angled lens, to prevent perspective distortion at the horizon. It also permitted the images to more closely approximate what a viewer would see at the actual site if he or she turned in all directions to capture the panoramic view.

An Uncommon Interest In Further Experimentation

A photographer from the age of fifteen, Mel Buschert spent a number of years performing experimental work with aerial imagery. He became interested in panorama photography because he was frustrated by the inability of medium format cameras to capture anything but tiny sections of large scenes. He wished to explore panorama photography as a medium for making new statements about landscapes. His remarks about the technical nature of the art suggest it was not an easy transition from single image formats to the large scale sensibilities essential in making successful panoramas. Buschert had to completely rethink photography with respect to exposure and visual content in the new format in which he was working. The principal problems lay in the nature of colour film and its limited capacity to embrace the wide range of light values present in every panorama. This problem was intensified by the fact that there are few places on earth where light values change as dramatically as they do in a single mountain scene. A huge range of light has to be compensated for by camera control. The photographer learned that only certain conditions yielded light values that made it possible to capture a scene in a single panoramic image. He learned that early mornings and evenings were best. Rich sidelighting made it possible for image exposures to be held together by strong principal elements of composition. If the light wasn't just right, or the colour range of the subject didn't fall within well defined limits, the image would fail. Buschert also found himself fighting the common misconception that panoramas must be taken from summits. He found that the best scenes were composed of mountains leaning tightly in around the camera, enclosing it as it would a viewer suddenly stepping from a car into a stunning scene. This knowledge came slowly. There were disappointments and expensive failures. For each mistake he made, the panorama camera would eat an entire roll of film. It took as many as eighteen visits to some of the sites to capture the right light, colour, and composition. Often intense cold caused the film to tear or shatter. Heavy equipment was lugged to the summits, or hauled about, suspended by special gyro-controlled mounts under helicopters. Mr. Buschert paid dearly for his art. It took five years to capture the images for this book.

A Capturable Immensity

The photographer learned a great deal about these landscapes as he explored their component elements of light and colour. Because the broad range of exposure in each of the images did not permit the use of polarization screens or filters, Buschert captured the Rockies as they really are. It should be a happy discovery for anyone living in this crowded and often polluted world to know that skies in the Rockies are still deep and truly blue. It should be comforting to know that wilderness of this vastness and magnitude still exists, and that it is easily and safely accessible to anyone interested enough to go there.

A Respectful Sense Of The Earth

The photographer who took the photographs in this book has lived a long time in these mountains. For him, the peaks stand on end, exposing a rich and magical history extending back to when the earliest oceans washed over a much different and younger planet. The camera, in imitation of the eye, chooses to see at exactly that light frequency which makes the world appear most opaque. Thus, the images organize reflections from the hardest reality of our existence. But behind each of these famous panoramas are the softer details of man's interaction with the mountains and the gradual realization of their enormous value as sacred places in a constantly changing world. The essays that accompany these images tell human stories which made the Rockies a celebrated backdrop to Canadian culture. Viewed together, we hope the pictures and the essays will marry experimental photography with living history, and that the resulting couple will be welcome at any gathering attended by those with a deep, respectful sense of the earth.

Robert Sandford
Banff, Canada
February, 1987

Mt. Brewster (2859 m)

Mt. Norquay (2522 m)

Sulphur Mtn. (2297 m)

Sawback Range

Mt. Temple (3543 m)

Pilot Mtn.

(2935 m)

Sulphur Mtn. (gondola viewpoint)

Mt. Brewster (2859 m)

Mt. Norquay (2522 m)

Sulphur Mtn. (2297 m)

Sulphur Mtn. (gondola viewpoint)

Sawback Range

Mt. Temple (3543 m)

Pilot Mtn.

(2935 m)

Mt. Rundle (2949 m)

Fairholme Ran

BANFF   11:20

Often the camera cannot be placed on a ground location to give the best view. I found it necessary to build a gyro-controlled mount that allows the panorama camera to hang 40 feet below the helicopter. The camera is very close to the cliff face in this panorama and it would have been impossible to climb to this position and use a tripod. The gyro mount was the ideal solution for this panorama to show Banff among the surrounding peaks.

BANFF FROM SULPHUR MOUNTAIN

The First National Park

In 1880 western Canada was still very much a wilderness. For two centuries Europeans had been pitting themselves against the fantastic size of the continent. Grand plans for the construction of a national railway were underway, but the west was still untilled prairie and wildly vertical peaks. Something very like a war was being waged against this unknown country, for pioneers were weary of the remoteness of the west. Their notion of paradise included the vision of a cultivated garden of agricultural wealth. This vision was opposed by the trackless barrens of the great plains and the indifferent cold of the high Rockies. Wilderness was something to be gobbled up, tamed, and if possible, civilized into the Victorian model of colonial pride. It is surprising, given the size of the country, that a small group of farsighted legislators and railway executives opted to protect some of the great wilderness by creating a national park. The resulting plan would have a resounding impact on Canada and Canadians for centuries.

Even during these pioneering years in the history of the colonial world, nature preserves were not a new idea. In 1885 two other national parks already existed in various stages of development. Yellowstone in Wyoming was the first in 1872, and Royal National Park followed shortly after when the Australian government set aside a rocky headland near the booming city of Sydney. Shrewdly citing these as examples, it was not solely wilderness preservation Cornelius Van Horne of the Canadian Pacific Railway had in mind when he urged the federal government to set aside Rocky Mountain National Reserve as Canada's first national park. It was apparent the railway needed to develop profitable ways to bring passengers to the west on the newly completed and under-utilized national railway. Van Horne envisioned one way to do this: build a chain of luxury hotels at the most spectacular places along the route. These places coincided nicely with the steepest passes over which the steam engines had to pull heavy coaches and dining cars. Within two years two other national parks were created, each strategically located along the line where steep right-of-ways and beautiful scenery combined to make hotels profitable and convenient. Three grand hotels were quickly constructed, the Banff Springs Hotel being the flagship of the group. Mt. Stephen House was located on the west side of the Great Divide just below the big hill to Kicking Horse Pass, when Yoho National Park was created in 1886. In the same year Glacier House was built in newly established Glacier National Park, on the summit of Rogers Pass. It was no longer necessary to haul heavy dining cars over these rugged sections of track. Clever and ultimately very profitable marketing in Europe and the eastern United States made the train ride through the Rockies and the Selkirks a must for that class of people who could afford to travel abroad and stay in first class hotels. The new status of these mountain parks also worked in favour of the railway. Under federal jurisdiction, development was controlled in these reserves and it was hard for competition to take hold. Though essential in the creation of the system, the building of railway hotels in the first national parks sowed a seed of conflict within the management structure of these resources that has yet to be resolved today.

Now there is much less unaltered wilderness in the Canadian west. The parks are suddenly precious to the Canadian psyche. Towns have grown within the parks, and new tensions have emerged, pitting developers against those who would have the parks remain wild. Not all decisions relating to the development of towns like Banff have been as farsighted as those made by the early politicans who legislated the park into existence. The town threatens to consume the valley. Fortunately, those who now stand for the preservation of the landscape are developing better ways to explain how these complex environments perpetuate themselves. If they are skillful in their arguments and do their research well, there is no reason why the town in this panorama should creep through the valley to totally usurp the view.

A century from now, when the world is more crowded and wilderness even more rare, it should still be possible to come here to find out what the world was like when forests were still primeval, and when travellers wandered valleys with no knowledge of what kind of country the wind was blowing from.

The Nation's Hot Tub

Siding 29 was much like any other railway siding when the tracks were first laid through the eastern Rockies in 1883. In that year significant copper and lead deposits were discovered thirty kilometres to the west, and a thousand people created Silver City overnight. In that same year, two railway workers saw vapours rising from the lower slopes of the mountain from which this panorama was taken. Local Indians directed Frank McCabe and William McCardell to a vent in the rock where steam from the soothing waters of a hot spring rose, curling to meet the cool mountain air. McCabe and McCardell squabbled over rights to the springs and the ensuing legal battle drew the attention of the federal government to the springs. After visiting the site in 1884, William Pearce, Superintendent of Mines, was able to convince the Minister of the Interior that the notion of a national reserve was a practical one, and that the springs would be a good place to start. Though McCabe and McCardell believed the legal settlement was inadequate, the government took deed to the land and in 1885 established a ten square mile reserve around the pool. Modelled after the American reserve at Hot Springs, Arkansas, the bath house facilities were leased to a private operator. The government, however, opted to remain in complete control of building design and service standards at the new facility. The reserve was expanded in 1887 to include 250 square miles (647 square kilometres) of surrounding mountain wilderness, and the reserve was gazetted as Rocky Mountains Park. By 1888 the Banff Springs Hotel was completed and international advertising began to draw the first visitors to the springs and the park. A town grew up near the 29th siding and was named Banff after the Scottish Banffshire, home of railway benefactors George Stephen and Donald Smith. At the same time, the enormous success of railway advertising had drawn a great deal of attention to these mountains. The published accounts of the first travellers beckoned a generation of climbers and adventurers west. It was absolutely true; they could simply get off the train and ascend unnamed and unclimbed peaks. In 1890 the railway built a small chateau at Lake Louise. Two years later, a fifty-one square mile reserve was established around the new chateau and the lake. The heyday of the outfitter and guide had begun.

Automobiles Are Banned

Banff was quickly becoming the major tourism destination of the day, a playground for the rich. Soon after the Banff Springs Hotel was completed, a pipeline was installed that took mineral water from the springs into the Brett Sanitarium, and word got out that the infirm could be healed in the therapeutic waters. By 1900 there were no fewer than eight luxury hotels in the thriving little town. Soon the town had electricity. Logging and mining were still permitted in the park, but Superintendent George Stewart hoped one day to replace the revenues from these by developing appropriate visitor attractions instead. As a start, thousands of trees were planted in a beautification program to replace forests burned during the building of the railway. Carriage roads were developed to Lake Minnewanka, Sundance Canyon, and the strange "hoodoos" left behind in the eroding glacial till of the valley. A boat house was built on the Bow River. An animal paddock, a zoo, and a museum were next. Coal mining was permitted in the park to ensure a reliable source of fuel for the passing trains. In 1902 the park was expanded to nearly twice its present size, and encompassed the watersheds of the Bow, Red Deer, Kananaskis and Spray rivers. It was one of the largest parks in the world, but the expansion proved difficult to manage. In 1911, the park shrunk again to a size its small staff could handle. By then the issue of the auto was looming, and a lot of old-timers were predicting the park was about to change.

The first "thunder wagon" rattled its way into the park in the summer of 1904. Using the railway right-of-way to guide them, often driving on the tracks, a Boston couple managed to drive from Calgary to Banff in less than a day. The appearance of this threatening new technology amused neither the railway nor the large number of liverymen and outfitters that for twenty years had supplied horses to the dudes who stayed at the hotel. By 1905 their combined lobby had effectively banned cars from the park on the grounds that they disturbed wildlife. Soon automobile owners were knocking again at the park gates. This technology would not go away. Automobiles were common on the Calgary-Banff coach road by 1911. By 1915 they were in the park, cruising along Banff Avenue at a maximum of 15 miles per hour. The day of the elite visitor was over. You no longer needed to take the train to Banff.

We Thought We Had Delirium Tremens

The age of the automobile burst quickly upon Banff. Road construction programs bit heavily into park budgets as increasing demands for new roads changed the very purpose and function of the national park system. A new style of visitor was on the road and his new independence demanded expanded facilities all over the park. The hotel systems were quick to react to the increased visitor potential. The Banff Springs, in particular, adapted quickly to its new role. The hotel had grown from a modest pre-1900 wooden structure to a strikingly grand hotel. The Great War had changed things, too. It drained Europe of its riches and bore with it a decade of people trying to forget. The twenties were a zany period in Banff's history. People were looking for fun at any cost. In 1925 an old railway worker happened into Banff. His description of the Banff Springs Hotel sums up the era:

"The truth is that I could not take beautiful Banff seriously. I dreamed it, and like so many dreams it was at once absurd and beautiful. On a pine-covered bank ... above the crystal foam of the Bow I came to a giant castle. It had no business being there, for when I was thereabouts so long ago, no one could have thought of it. The dream castle was full ... of people who talked all at once and I saw in a moment that they were not real. If any of us workers of the old days had seen their likes we should have thought we had delirium tremens."

Still Timeless Under Azure Skies

In 1930 the National Parks Act of Canada composed a unique system of seventeen parks across the nation. As a result of this legislation, Rocky Mountains Park was renamed Banff after the town, and its boundaries were reduced to roughly their present limits. Through the depression and the Second World War, roads continued to expand slowly into the wilderness. The end of the war brought new prosperity, rising incomes, and a demand for new cars. Until the mid-fifties, most Banff businessmen closed for the winter. They smeared Bon Ami soap over their windows and went away for the cold months as soon as the snow buried the campgrounds and the hiking trails. The discovery of new oil in Alberta, however, brought more prosperity and nearby Calgary was bound to grow. With affluence, new recreational patterns would emerge and the park would change, too. The little town of Banff would forego its seasonal sleep.

Skiing in the Canadian Rockies made its first appearance in Banff in the 1920s. Climbing guides hired by the CP hotels stayed on for the winter to teach locals how to ski. (Until the advent of skis, snowshoeing was considered the only civilized way to walk across the snow.) A ski club was started in Banff, and members established a small area on a mountain near the town. By the early 1930s small lodges were established above Lake Louise and in the watershed of Sunshine Creek near Banff. The locals slowly realized that skiing was a very suitable reaction to the long Canadian winters. Soon after, they discovered that the mountains were at least as beautiful in winter as they were during the warmer months. By the mid-1950s ski trains began arriving weekly in the winter, loaded with eastern Canadians anxious to try their skills at Banff's three fledgling ski areas. By 1968 the ski areas were big business in Banff and even the prestigious Banff Springs Hotel was open all year round.

In 1959 Sulphur Mountain Gondola Lift Ltd. introduced yet another option for visitors on a short stay in Canada's first national park. They built a gondola to the summit of Sulphur Mountain, the same mountain from which the famous hot springs emerged. From the summit, where gondolas enter the white fortress of the upper station, the viewer is confronted with a panorama that was backdrop for the early human history of the park. In the far distance is the route the trains take into the Rockies. The railway has given rise to gift shops, restaurants and apartment buildings. Staff accommodations are filled with young people having a good time living in this busy resort town. Banff huddles beneath the ice-smoothed nub of Tunnel Mountain. An early railway survey crew once considered tunnelling through it to lay the tracks into the heart of the Rockies. Mount Rundle towers, overthrust and barren, above the valley. Just out of view are the hot springs where the national parks legacy began. Directly below is the modern Banff Springs Hotel, gracefully aloof and imposing above Bow Falls. A grand castle that reached completion in 1928, it remains the single most popular visitor attraction in the park. An architectural wonder even today, it is valued at more than fifty million dollars. But we forget why we came. Beyond the hotel and the town, ranges of blue-grey peaks, lakes and silent forests remain timeless under azure skies.

Fairview Mtn. (2744 m)

Mt. St. Piran

LAKE LOUISE   9:50

Reflections are always fascinating. The Chateau has more dimension with the addition of the reflection. The exposure is on the limits of this film. The extremes of dark shadow and brittle white glacier called for an exposure biased towards the glacier. The peaks surrounding the lake just received a fresh snowfall and the sky was perfectly clear.

Chateau Lake Louise

Mt. Niblock (2976 m)

The Beehive (2270 m)

Mt. Whyte (2983 m)

Mt. Victoria (3464 m)

Mt. Lefroy (3423 m)

LAKE LOUISE

A Tear In The Stone Curtain

If any one place can symbolize the aesthetic of the Canadian Rockies it is Lake Louise, by far the most famous and most heavily visited natural feature in these mountains. No matter how many times one visits this shoreline, it is impossible not to be stunned by the immediacy of the renowned view. Even the most jaded traveller cannot fail to be impressed with what the V-shaped opening at the end of the lake exposes. A tear in the great stone curtain reveals the very heart of the Rockies. Not only is Mt. Victoria a huge mountain (11,365 feet, nearly 3800 metres), it is draped splendidly in ancient ice. Six glaciers flow or fall into the narrow valley below its awesome face. It is the outflow of these glaciers that creates Lake Louise.

All the major forces that fashioned this landscape are mirrored in the lake's blue waters. Above and to the left of the lake is Fairview Mountain. Its thick bands of stratified stone reveal the marine origins of these mountains. The huge relief of Mt. Victoria testifies to the power of the tectonic forces that pushed this ancient sea floor two miles into the sky. The deep glaciers of the upper Victoria Glacier are mute evidence of how moving ice added shape and new relief to the aging mountains. The long moraines that fill the Plain of Six Glaciers amply prove how time, wind, water, and ice wear away even the tallest peaks. The Rockies are hip deep in their own rubble.

Man has been a part of this scene only briefly. His monument, the elegant Chateau Lake Louise, stands on an old moraine at the edge of the lake. This railway hotel has figured largely in the developing reputation of the Rockies. Without the Chateau, the lake would not be as famous.

A Railway Opens The Way

To the first explorers, the Rockies were not beautiful. They were dangerous and unpredictable. Tangled forests and unnamed, unknown valleys were mazes requiring decades to explore. If anything, the mountains were enormous obstacles demanding grit and determination from pilgrims in their westward search for the Pacific coast. It was not until people could travel safely and comfortably through them, that these mountains assumed a grandeur worthy of celebration abroad.

Canada could ill-afford the great railway it undertook to build in 1881. The country had a small population and an uncertain claim over remote regions of the uninhabited plains. When construction started west from Montreal, railway executives had no firm idea of a route the rails would take through the five ranges of mountains dividing the prairies from the sea. Whatever the path, it had to satisfy a number of critical conditions. It had to be far enough south to protect

Canadian sovereignty in the slowly developing west, it required low grades leading up to the mountain passes, and it had to be operational even in winter. Nor was there time to spare in establishing a viable route. If British Columbia was to remain part of confederation, it had to be connected to the rest of Canada with steel. To this end, legions of surveyors were dispatched ahead of construction crews in search of an appropriate passage to the coast.

In 1881 the Canadian Pacific Railway appointed Major A. B. Rogers chief engineer of its Mountain Division. His was the monumental task of somehow connecting the railway that was advancing quickly across the prairies, to the east, and up the Fraser Valley from the Pacific, to the west. There were nearly a thousand kilometers, almost six hundred miles, of wilderness between the two converging lines. This wilderness was composed of dense forests, unexplored peaks, bare rock, and ice.

Major Rogers was a gruff and fierce man. Only by driving his horses and his men did he finally succeed in finding a reasonable path through the great stone wall that threatened westward progress. En route, he and his men made other discoveries.

As the Rockies did not grant easy passage, surveyors often spent months in the same place. While seeking brief respite from long hours of bushwacking and the backbreaking task of locating a right-of-way through the resisting rock, they explored neighbouring valleys and peaks. The lucky ones, like Tom Wilson, were led by Indian guides to favourite fishing and hunting grounds bordering the big valleys favoured as routes for the tracks.

After obtaining an honourable discharge from the North West Mounted Police in April of 1881, Tom Wilson hired on as a horse packer with Rogers' crew. That summer he helped survey a route through the eastern Rockies as far west as the Great Divide. In the spring of 1882, he was back, this time packing supplies to survey crews on the

British Columbia side of Kicking Horse Pass.

During a stretch of bad weather in August of that year, Wilson met a small band of Stoney Indians east of the pass. Huddled around a campfire in the rain, they heard the thunder of avalanches above them in the mist. By way of sign language, one of the Indians indicated to Wilson that the thunder was coming from a "snow mountain above the lake of the little fishes." This man, whose Indian name meant "money-seeker" or "gold-seeker" in English, responded favourably to Wilson's request to guide him to the lake in the thundering valley above them. On August 24, 1882, Edwin Goldseeker guided the first white man to the shores of Lake Louise. Wilson's guide also indicated the presence of two smaller lakes above the "lake of the little fishes." One, he explained, was called the "goat's looking glass," as mountain goats were known to frequent its shores and had been seen peering into the still water. The other later became known as Lake Agnes.

Wilson, mightily impressed with his discovery, named the lake of little fishes Emerald Lake. It appeared, thusly named, on the first geological map ever made of this region of the Rockies.

In October of 1883, the railway was advancing up the Bow Valley. It is apparent other railway workers visited the lake in this and each of the subsequent years. After all, the lake was well known for good fishing. In 1883 the lake was viewed by members of the British Association for the Advancement of Science, led by Sir Richard Temple. Temple was travelling with his daughter and was guided by Tom Wilson. A story has emerged that Wilson renamed the lake for Louise, Sir Richard's daughter. In fact, it was named for Princess Louise Caroline Alberta, the fourth daughter of Queen Victoria. She was also the wife of the Marquis of Lorne, who was then Governor-General of Canada. Oddly enough, Princess Louise never visited the magnificent lake named in her honour.

The First Fatality In North American Climbing

The successful completion of the railway on November 7, 1885, did not bring to an end the problems facing the CPR. The cost of constructing the mountain sections of the railroad had nearly bankrupt the country and caused the downfall of at least one government. One way the railway could help pay for itself was by developing a system of tourist class hotels along its route. The sumptuous Banff Springs Hotel was completed in the spring of 1888. Grand hotels were planned and built in Field and at the summit of Rogers Pass. A more modest chalet was completed on the shores of Lake Louise and opened in the spring of 1890. Early advertising promoted the small hotel as a centre for mountaineering and outdoor adventure. By now, word was out to the rest of the world that unnamed and unclimbed peaks rose in every direction from the spectacular rail line that pierced the very centre of the Rockies. It wasn't long before climbers were disembarking from the trains in hopes of achieving a foothold on the shining summits.

Prominent among the first alpinists in the Rockies was a group of Americans. Samuel Allen, a Freshman at Yale, had been introduced to the notion of exploring the Rockies by his mother who visited them in 1889. When he came to Lake Louise by way of the California Sierras in 1891, the CPR was just then completing a road to the chalet on the shore. Allen was very much taken by what he saw, and two years later returned with Walter Wilcox, a companion from Yale. The chalet had burned down in 1892, so the two camped in tents on the shore of the lake. During their brief stay, they made unsuccessful attempts to climb Mt. Victoria and Mt. Temple. En route they caught the first glimpses of other spectacular valleys adjacent to the lake. That winter, back at Yale, they planned a better equipped and more ambitious expedition and in 1894 returned, bringing other Yale students along.

The Yale Lake Louise Club explored much of the Lake Louise area, discovering Paradise Valley, Sentinel Pass, Moraine and Consolation Lakes. Their key contribution, however, was that they went home and wrote about it. Their climbing stories, and the fine book by Wilcox would bring thousands to the shore of the fabled lake.

In 1895 twenty members of the Boston-based Appalachian Mountain Club arrived at Lake Louise. Among this group was its president, Charles Fay, as well as Charles Thompson and Philip S. Abbot. That summer, they tried unsuccessfully to climb Mt. Lefroy. The following winter, Abbot, obsessed with this mountain, made elaborate plans for its ascent. In 1896 the party returned. Staying at the new chalet, they rose at 5:00 a.m., and on August 3rd proceeded to the toe of the glacier. By 5:30 p.m., after much cutting of steps in the snow, they were within seventy-five feet of the summit. Before them, however, loomed a steep and shattered wall. Leading on this difficult pitch, Abbot fell backwards, headfirst onto the snow below and rolled downslope with the rope coiling about him. Tragically, he died before his friends could help. Two days later, a rescue party composed of Tom Wilson, George Little, Charles Fay and hotel manager Willoughby Astley, recovered Abbot's body. Abbot's death was the first in North American mountaineering. A public outcry went up about the validity of the sport. On the first anniversary of Abbot's death, a large expedition led by Fay successfully completed the first ascent of Mt. Lefroy. They made their way via Abbot Pass, named for their deceased friend in honour of his part in the history of these peaks. The next day they climbed the big peak at the furthest end of the lake and, because it was the Jubilee year of the Queen, named it and the glacier for Queen Victoria.

The controversy surrounding Abbot's death focused more attention on the Rockies, and Lake Louise was right in the centre of it. Unscaled peaks extended in every direction from the lake, and climbers from everywhere in the world took the train to claim them. The small chalet gradually grew into an elegant, large hotel, and the CPR imported Swiss alpine guides to the Rockies to ensure that guests survived to pay their bills.

New Summits

Changes in the hotel have mirrored public interest in Lake Louise. In 1890, when the first chalet-style hotel was built, it was still difficult to reach the lake. A rough trail gave way to a road in 1893, when a slightly larger lodge was under construction to replace the first building destroyed by fire the year before. As railway advertising drew more and more people, a regular station was built in the valley floor below. In 1899 the construction of a Tudor-influenced chateau made it possible for even more people to stay in the area. This development, combined with the growing reputation of the Banff Springs Hotel, established the reputation of the Rockies as an internationally famous vacation destination. Chateau Lake Louise was so popular it had to be expanded again to meet the needs of climbers and hikers that came from everywhere to drink in the legend. Walter Painter, the architect who would later redesign the Banff Springs Hotel, came to Lake Louise to design a 350 bed extension to the hotel. Construction of this giant cement wing and a tramway up from the valley began in 1912. In 1913 the new wing, dwarfing the original chateau, was opened. It featured a ballroom one hundred and eighty feet long. Needless to say, the hotel was the last word in comfort.

During the First World War a road was constructed from Banff to Lake Louise. In 1922 increased mountaineering activity on Mt. Lefroy and Mt. Victoria necessitated that a hut be built at the summit of Abbot Pass. The building of this structure required that materials be carried up the lower Victoria Glacier by horse and then manhandled up Death Trap col to the pass. The resulting stone structure became the highest building in Canada. Everything pointed to endless prosperity. At least until July of 1924.

The extensive use of local wood in construction presented a high fire hazard in mountain hotels. The remote nature of the Chateau demanded unusual diligence against the hazard, for if a fire started, staff would be hard pressed to put it out. The nearest fire engines were in Banff, an hour and a half away. The fire that broke out in the old section of the Chateau at about 2:00 p.m. on July 3, 1924 started on the third floor of the staff quarters and spread quickly to engulf the entire north wing. An hour later the old wing collapsed on itself, totally destroyed. The staff lost everything they owned. The hotel adjusted quickly. By 6:00 p.m. dinner was served as usual for the 126 guests in the Painter wing, followed by dancing until eleven. The next day, valet, shoeshine and hairdressing services were restored as though nothing had happened. By a remarkable feat of construction engineering, a new wing matching the Painter complex was completed by May of the following year.

The new hotel was not particularly beautiful. Jon Whyte, author of a book on the history of the lake, commented that it was a "hotel meant to be looked from rather than a hotel to be looked at." Many others commented on how much more it looked like a prison than a hotel. Not until 1984 did the building get a new facade, something desperately needed to make the hotel fit attractively into its striking setting. In 1987 a new wing was added to the hotel.

The Lake Louise area is still an important centre for mountaineering. A new generation of highly experienced and well equipped climbers make ascents of these mountains by new and more dangerous routes. The village of Lake Louise, the town of Field to the west, and nearby Banff are well populated by climbers and guides attracted still to the serene and awesome beauty of Lake Louise.

Moraine Creek Valley

Tower of Babel (2360 m)

Mt. Bowlen/Yamnee (307 4 m)

Mt. Little/Nom (3140 m)

3054 m)

MORAINE LAKE   10:20

This very rugged area is one of the most interesting in the
Rockies. The large rock pile which forms the edge of the lake
is an ideal location for photographers. The greatest problem
is to find a location where the trees in the foreground do not
obstruct the image.

Deltaform Mtn./Saknowa (3424 m)

Mt. Tuzo/Sagowa (3245 m)

Mt. Perren/Sa[...]

Mt. Allen/Shappee

(3310 m)

Neptuak Mtn. (3237 m)

Moraine Lake Lodge

Moraine Lake

MORAINE LAKE

The Ten On The Back Of The Twenty

The Great Divide region encompassing Lake Louise is undoubtedly one of the most densely beautiful landscapes in the world. Indeed, Lake Louise would not be so famous if the surrounding region did not enclose other spectacular features. Nearby Moraine Lake draws almost as many visitors annually as Lake Louise, and with good reason. So prominent is Moraine Lake in the Canadian psyche, that it has been featured repeatedly in advertising campaigns promoting the Canadian Rockies. For decades a photograph of the lake and the Valley of the Ten Peaks has graced the back of the Canadian twenty dollar bill; a subtle reminder, perhaps, of the extent to which tourism in the Rockies contributes to the national economy.

Moraine Lake, discovered by Walter Wilcox and his climbing companions, was named for the large, apparently glacial, moraine that long ago dammed the water of Moraine Creek to form the lake. A student at Yale University, Wilcox and a few friends had spent their summers exploring unnamed valleys and peaks adjacent to the Canadian Pacific Railway right-of-way. Wilcox notes that when they started their explorations, what they didn't know about mountaineering could have filled several books. They were young, however, and had much courage. In

1894, after reading a few notes in a climbing book, they departed from Lake Louise to attempt a first ascent of Mt. Lefroy. Though disaster accompanied this expedition, the climbers miraculously survived. This first perilous and unsuccessful attempt on the mountain foreshadowed an accident two years later when Philip Abbot became the first fatality in the history of North American climbing. Repeated exposure to the dangers of the mountain made a deep impact on young Walter. In subsequent years Wilcox developed highly refined mountaineering skills and made many first ascents in the Rockies. He also explored hundreds of square miles of virtually unknown mountain terrain. Books about his adventures became increasingly popular, and through them many would feel the irresistable urge to see these peaks with their own eyes. In 1899 Wilcox was already famous when he stood at last on the shores of Moraine Lake, a beautiful tarn he'd spotted on his first ascent of Mt. Temple. The weather was bad the day Wilcox decided to take a walk up the valley:

"I walked about a mile and a half and came to a ravine where a roaring cascade, encumbered with logs and great boulders comes out of the valley to the south-east. I got across on a slippery log and after another mile, came to a massive pile of stones, where the water gurgles as it rushes along in subterranean channels. Ascending a ridge about fifty feet high, there lay before me one of the most beautiful lakes that I have ever seen. This lake, which I called "Moraine Lake" from the ridge of glacial formation at its lower end, is about a mile and a half long."

His companion, S. E. S. Allen, consulted local Indians and outfitter Tom Wilson about Indian words and gave each of the peaks a Stoney name for its place in the sequence of the ten. The names have a magical ring. Sweeping the first vista from left to right he named Heejee the first, Nom the second, Yamnee the third, then Tonsa, Sapta, Shappee, Sagowa, Saknowa, Neptuak, and the tenth, Wenkchemna. Some of these names have since been changed and each of the peaks has been climbed. Recent geological surveys of the lake's shore have also yielded a different idea of how the lake was formed. Wilcox may have been incorrect in his assumption that the ridge of debris damming the lake was of glacial origin. The shattered rock appears to have been part of a rock slide that came down from the Tower Of Babel.

The panorama was taken from the top of the moraine where Wilcox must have stood for his first view of the lake. To the left of the image is the Moraine Creek valley and the forest Wilcox likely thrashed his way through to find the ridge of shattered boulders that dam the perfect blue of the lake's glacial waters. The great stone bulk at the centre of the panorama is the base of the Tower Of Babel, an immense pillar popular with rock climbers. Sweeping down from the pillar is a wide cone of broken scree caused by frost shattering of the soft sedimentary strata that compose the mountains in this entire scene. Above and behind the lake are nine of the ten peaks for which the valley has been named. The tenth, Wenkchemna, is out of site behind the towering shoulder of Mt. Temple. The boat dock, the pleasant lodge hidden in the trees, and the parking lot behind the viewer are the few suggestions that the lake has changed since Wilcox found it.

Needles Of The Golden Larch

The history of European exploration in the Rockies is so brief and so recent that the feats of the first climbers are but trailheads from which visitors can start on their own adventures among the high peaks. Unlike the Alps, where trails cross every pass and villages dot even the remotest valleys, the main ranges of these stupendous mountains are wilderness. Good trails advance over many of the most important passes, but spirited walkers can still find themselves alone in very wild country in an hour's hike from any major highway. Some of the finest walking in all of Canada's mountain parks is in the vicinity of Moraine Lake.

One of the most famous trails in the Canadian Rockies begins at the ridge of broken rock Walter Wilcox used as his first lookout when he discovered the lake. Along the shore to the right of the lake, it wanders through a pleasant forest of lodgepole pine and white spruce, past the last cabins that cluster around Moraine Lake Lodge. Wide and well-surfaced, it begins the switchback ascent of the lower shoulder of Mt. Temple. As the trail climbs, the slope of the ridge takes the hiker gradually away from the water. Soon the lake below is a distant stunning blue. In July, when the snow melts from the shadowed forests above the lake, flowers of a thousand hues sway back and forth in the gentle breezes that blow across the divide. There are wild orchids, lavender and white against the spruce needles of the forest floor. Higher, the Indian paintbrushes blossom scarlet in glades that open up near timberline as the trail completes its six hundred metre ascent of the ridge. Three kilometres from the lake, the larches appear, their needles in summer a faint and pale green, soft like moss and delicate against the black bark of branches and gnarled trunks. In autumn the needles burn yellow-gold in radiantly clear air. At a junction near the top of the ridge, the trail narrows and winds into Larch Valley. Simply a narrow plateau below two huge peaks, this valley encompasses one of the most dense stands of larch trees in the park. It is a rite in autumn, when the whole ridge turns gold, to visit these trees. On weekends late in September, when the frost has fallen hard and often on mountains blue in the oblique light, pilgrims march in long lines up into the trees. After resting in the meadow beneath branches heavy with golden needles, they often carry on past the ragged treeline and up the steep switchbacks to Sentinel Pass. Little more than five kilometres from the lake, this high and windy col is the highest point to which trails wander in this part of the Rockies. Beyond here only climbers go. At more than 2600 metres, the view from the col offers a grand panorama of the Valley of the Ten Peaks and, to the north, breathtaking glimpses of the rocky sentinels that shoot skyward from a shoulder of Pinnacle Peak. Far below, the forest creeps to the head of Paradise Valley. Distant and unseen behind the massive bulk of the Mitre lies Lake Louise.

And Stones Shaped Like Eagles Landing

Larch Valley is only one of the destinations along the trail that climbs the ridge above and to the right of the lake. If, instead of turning up into the larches, one continues along the crest of the ridge, the forest soon opens into grand views of the upper valley. Once the end of the lake is passed, the trail winds slowly upward into vast fells of glacially strewn boulders, the way bright with wildflowers. Soon a small tarn, barely ice-free in August, presents itself amidst a rock-tumble of talus and ancient glacier debris where the slicing whistle of the marmot is broadcast to the wind. Eiffel Lake is a good place to compare human scale to the bolder dimensions of surrounding peaks and passes. This lake was not formed like most alpine lakes. Instead of lying in a basin carved out of bedrock by the advance and retreat of glacial ice, Eiffel Lake lies in a hollow created when a massive rockslide broke away from Neptuak and buried much of the valley. All around you is a jumble of house-sized rocks. The horizon is stone, reeling in a dizzying circle two kilometres above the valley floor. Walter Wilcox stood here, too, and felt the same humbling awe:

> "It would be difficult to find another lake of small size in a wilder setting, the shores being of great angular stones, perfectly in harmony with the wild range of mountains beyond. Except in one place where a green and inviting slope comes down to the water, this rough ground is utterly unsuitable for vegetation and nearly devoid of trees."

Still the trail pushes on. Rising and falling through more hostile terrain, the path soon leaves the flowers behind. If you are not careful you can lose the way completely amidst the broken rocks that rise along the shoulder of Wenkchemna Pass. Wenkchemna, the last of the ten peaks, rises brutally above a narrow gap that forms the pass between it and Neptuak, the Stoney nine. From the summit of Wenkchemna Pass, you look down a deep defile into the cold stone and glacial ice on the west side of the Great Divide. One more step and you are in another province, another park. Most often, hikers stop here. It is a steep walk down the defile. At the base of the pass, in a remote corner where Banff, Yoho, and Kootenay parks join, is the Eagle's Eyrie. Sculpted by wind and water and time, this great stone bird appears to be hovering above a rocky nest.

No Place For Ladies

At the time when Wilcox and his pals were wandering all over the Great Divide of the Rockies, it was generally agreed that women were neither interested in, nor capable of climbing mountains. Though a few women climbers had already proven they were more than capable of enduring what men could in pursuit of summits, the Canadian west was still a man's land. Women were simply not expected to participate in serious mountaineering expeditions. Except for pleasant chatter around the campfire at night, they were considered a burden on the trail. It was not long, however, before these sexist notions were forced to change. Agnes Macdonald certainly cocked a few eyebrows by demanding a ride on the cow catcher of a passenger train through the Rockies. But she was expected to be a little eccentric. As the wife of the Prime Minister of Canada, she could do whatever she liked.

The woman who really blew the theory apart was Mary Sharples. The daughter of wealthy Quaker parents, young Mary first came to the Rockies in 1888. She accompanied her school companion, Mary Vaux, on a summer holiday to Glacier House where Vaux's brothers were doing research on the Illecillewaet Glacier. The following summer she returned again, but with a new name. She had married Dr. Charles Schäffer, a botanist who studied alpine flora in the Rocky Mountains. It appears that during her first visits to this area, she acted quite predictably; she announced her dislike for the crude conditions of the bush and made it clear that this was no way for civilized folk to travel. It was clear, too, from Mary's early journals that she was quite prepared to relegate the backcountry to the exclusive domain of men:

"We fretted for the strength of man, for the way was long and hard, and only the tried and stalwart might venture where cold and heat, starvation and privation stalked ever at the explorer's heels. In meek despair we bowed our head to the inevitable, to the cutting knowledge of the superiority of the endurance of man . . . . They left us sitting on the railway track following them with hungry eyes as they plunged into the distant hills . . ."

Her husband met an untimely death in 1903 and, out of love for his work, Mary did outstanding watercolour paintings and photographs for a book on alpine flora that was published in 1907.

During her early visits to the Lake Louise area, Mary developed a close association with Tom Wilson. It was Wilson who supplied Mary and her friend Mollie Adams with horses and a guide to take them to Moraine Lake in 1904. The trip to Moraine Lake changed Mary's attitude about the dangers and hardships of the backcountry. It also marked the start of her numerous backcountry explorations. Returning year after year, the two woman acquired experience and good backcountry skills. By 1906 their forays had taken them as far north as Wilcox Pass and the Columbia Icefield. In 1907 Schäffer, Adams, and guide Billy Warren made an even longer journey to Fortress Lake. In July of 1908 Schäffer, again with Billy Warren, found Maligne Lake and opened up some of the most spectacular backcountry in what had become Jasper National Park. At last, a women earned an honourable place in the history of the Rockies.

A Consolation Prize

Wilcox first sighted Moraine Lake and the Valley of the Ten Peaks from the slopes of Mount Temple during an unsuccessful attempt at the summit. He and Samuel Allen saw this scene again, a year later, from the summit of Mount Temple, the highest point yet attained in the Canadian Rockies. Now, using the tourist route, Mt. Temple can be climbed with just an ice axe and good strong legs. By retracing young Walter's steps up from Sentinel Pass, one can see the scene as it was spread out before him on the 18th of August, 1894. At noon he and Samuel Allen looked down through the smoke haze from distant forest fires, at an ocean of frozen wave-like peaks that radiated to the horizon in every direction. From the high and windy summit, they looked upon the limitless barrens of "a narrow secluded valley with a small lake enclosed by wild rugged precipices — a scene of awesome desolation." During his later explorations with Ross Peecock he named them Desolation Valley and Moraine Lake. Exploring further, they followed a stream to another valley, so pleasant in contrast to the desolate upper reaches beyond Moraine Lake that, on Peecock's suggestion, they called it the Consolation Valley, and the lake bears the same name. From the shore of Moraine Lake it is a gentle hour's walk to Consolation, no small prize for those with little time to enter the heart of these peaks.

Yoho Valley

Yoho River

Kicking Horse River

MEETING-OF-THE-WATERS 11:20

This view of the river is only visible by climbing out onto
steep boulders along the edge. With the constant roar of
the water and the unbalanced position on top of a sloping
rock face, it was difficult to appreciate the surroundings.
When the camera was firmly secure and the exposure made,
the beauty of the area became evident and proved well
worth the effort.

Cathedral Crags (3073 m)

Kicking Horse River

Mt. Ogden (2695 m)

THE MEETING-OF-THE-WATERS

An Ultimate Awe

The earliest travellers used few words to describe their rugged, violent world, for they were hunters, alone and at hazard in a savage land. Their words were simple, powerful symbols for what they saw. The word used most often amidst the rock walls and the waterfalls was one of wonder, a simple word for awe — Yoho.

For ten thousand years men made only infrequent visits to the heart of these wild mountains. The winters were long and bitter; travel was difficult through the deep snows. Although there was wonder with each day's dawn, these were precarious places, for there was also great hazard. The land was indifferent to life, and even the heartiest, bravest soul would find new ways to perish in the long cold of winter.

In the middle of the last century a small group of curious men straggled timidly over an unnamed and rock-walled pass. They stood in awe of the endless ranges of new mountains that tumbled forever to the west. The year was 1858. Seeking to measure the untold vastness of the new land, the Palliser Expedition experienced Yoho. These men learned quickly the hazards of travel through the timber-choke of narrow valleys. One lesson was nearly fatal. A horse kicked Sir James Hector, the party's leader, and he nearly died. Though they suffered, they recorded the wonder they saw and wandered, for a time, by rivers they named, and through valleys that would soon hear the thunder of the passing trains.

Subsequent travellers have felt this same awe for the deep gorges and rumbling waters of the Yoho and Kicking Horse Valleys. These are imposing places. The west side of the Great Divide receives more rain than the peak-shielded front ranges farther to the east. The forests are dark jungles of spruce and pine that can swallow travellers for days on end. Water is everywhere. Creeks and streams pour out of every forest, and rivers fall from high snowfields over cliff faces into fern-alive woods in the shadowed valleys. It is here we find Canada's tallest falls, "Takakkaw", the Indians called it, "it is magnificent." It cascades four hundred metres down a great wall just a short distance from the meeting of these two famous rivers. Even with roads into them, these remain wild, challenging peaks. It is hard to imagine why, barely a century ago, our fledgling nation decided to push the longest railway ever built, through these valleys.

The prevailing mood in Canada in 1870 was one of optimism. Feeling the spirit and vision of youth, Canada, in its first decade, set out to expand its boundaries from sea to sea. In 1871 the Dominion promised British Columbia a railroad if it joined the proud confederation. The promise nearly bankrupt the land. Though the hard rock of the Canadian Shield offered tough resistance to the advancing rails, the prairies were quick to fall beneath the spell of rumbling engines and the eerie wail of a steam whistle on a cold night. The mountains posed the ultimate challenge to early railway builders. The monumental resistance they offered to the advance of the ringing rails could not be easily overcome. The railway arrived in the Lake Louise area in 1883. The first real construction problems began when the route crossed Kicking Horse Pass. From the summit of the pass, the landscape literally plunged into the Kicking Horse Valley. For railway engineers, it was the first alarming look at the kind of topography they would have to contend with for several hundred miles. Sir Sanford Fleming visited the pass in 1883 to examine the difficulties his engineers were facing in what would become Yoho National Park. He walked the rail route into the valley.

"A series of precipices run sheer up from the boiling current to form a contracted canyon. A path has therefore been traced along the hillside, on the steep aclivity there is scarcely a foothold; nevertheless we have to follow for some miles this thread of a trail . . . I do not think that I could ever forget this terrible walk; it was the greatest trial I have ever experienced."

The initial roadbed followed a rather direct route into the valley at a steeper incline than the engineers would have liked. Their greatest fears were realized when the first trains careened dangerously down the grade. Out-of-control trains were so common that runaway lanes were installed at critical intervals along the track. A divisional point was established at the base of the hill to accommodate workers required to maintain the track and clean up in the event of a disaster. This divisional point became the town of Field, now the administrative centre of Yoho National Park. The steepness of the grade up to the pass made it necessary to drop heavy dining cars at the divisional point so the steam powered engines could pull to the summit. In order that passengers were still well served between these points, a hotel was built in Field by the Canadian Pacific Railway. Mt. Stephen House was a grand place. For years it was the centre of exploration for the new national park set aside in 1886. Intrepid easterners and aristocratic Europeans mounted horses to explore the valleys and hired local guides to take them to the summits of nearby peaks. Always they would stop at the Meeting-of-the-Waters, the thundering junction of the Yoho and Kicking Horse Rivers at the base of Kicking Horse Pass.

Early explorers of Yoho National Park were the same men who figured largely in opening the Lake Louise area to the awaiting world. Shortly after he discovered Lake Louise in August of 1882, Tom Wilson found himself in the area of Kicking Horse Pass. Extra horses he had left there wandered off to feed, and Wilson searched all the usual places he knew they frequented. Past the wide flats on the Kicking Horse River, where the town of Field would be soon located, he passed a natural stone bridge spanning a canyon on the river. This natural bridge is one of the most popular attractions in the park today. Wilson continued on the trail of the horses to where a small stream entered the Kicking Horse from the north. We can imagine him growing angry with the missing horses at this point, the still forests echoing with his curses. Beneath the unique face of Mt. Burgess the stream widened into a big pool that mirrored the reflections of the peaks crowded in around the edge of the lake. The lake rivalled Lake Louise in sheer, rugged beauty, and he called it Emerald Lake, the name he had first applied to the lake of the little fishes. Emerald is a good name for this lake, for it describes well the colour of the summer water. At the turn of the century the CPR built a small lodge there. After many decades of use, Emerald Lake Lodge fell into private hands and in the mid-1980's was completely renovated into an elegant resort.

In 1909 the CPR abandoned the direct route down the pass in favour of two corkscrew-shaped tunnels that wound the track gently down the summit at a grade engines could easily handle. But still trains are occasionally swept from the tracks by rockslides and avalanches that thunder like waterfalls down unbelievably steep mountains. It is no wonder the Canadian heritage has been closely tied to the building of this railroad. In Yoho that heritage is wound around long hills, steam engines, and tunnels cut spirally into the living rock. If it is possible to experience wonder, then this might be the place, for it is a wonder there is a railway here at all.

The first roads built in the park carried horse drawn "Tally-Hos" to scenic sites away from the railway right-of-way. The first of these carriage roads was constructed from Field to Emerald Lake in 1904. Other byways were eventually built to the Meeting-of-the-Waters and Takakkaw Falls in 1910. The first noisy automobiles did not find their way into the valley of the Kicking Horse until after the Great War. Records show that the National Parks Service bought its first vehicle, a one ton Ford truck, in 1919. In June of 1926 a motor road was extended from Lake Louise down the steep pass into Field. In the following year the road was completed through the canyon of the Kicking Horse to Golden. With roads extending into the park, the railway no longer monopolized access to the high peaks. The first year the roads opened to the park, 7,200 vehicles made their way over the rough and dusty roads into Field. By 1962 Canada's national highway retraced the route of the first tracks westward to the summit of Rogers Pass; another wild summit discovered and developed by the CPR. By that time more than one hundred thousand vehicles a year entered the spell of wonder beneath the Yoho peaks.

Since those early days, Yoho has been recognized for more than its unique place in the history of the railway. The rugged mountains have been a mecca for climbers since the railway first put the image of high Canadian peaks into the minds of visiting adventurers. The books published by early climbers not only detailed the wild beauty and grand summits, but also served as widespread advertising for further explorations of the Rockies. So popular was this small park in early climbing circles, that it became the site of the first annual camp of the newly formed Alpine Club of Canada in 1906. This famous camp is repeated every year in various parts of the Rocky and Selkirk mountains. It was this club that opened up much of Yoho for both summer and winter visitation.

Early explorations focused on the Lake O'Hara region, named for Lieutenant Colonel Robert O'Hara who visited the lake in 1887. In 1931, the Alpine Club purchased a lodge built by the CPR. Elizabeth Parker Hut on a tranquil meadow near the lake, and Lake O'Hara Lodge on the shoreline, attract climbers and hikers from everywhere in the world to the larch forests and clean air of one of Yoho's special places. Many aficionados claim O'Hara to be the place with the best views, the best climbing and the best trails in the Canadian Rockies. The water flowing from this famous lake joins the Kicking Horse just below the pass, contributing to the thunder of the river at the right of the panorama.

The Alpine Club also built facilities for mountaineers in the Little Yoho Valley. Stanley Mitchell Hut was constructed in 1941 for climbers and skiers anxious for access to the President Group, a rugged range of mountains bordering the Wapta Icefield which straddles the Great Divide between Banff and Yoho National Parks. Melt from an eastern tongue of this icefield forms Peyto Lake while melt from westerly flowing glaciers splashes into the Yoho River which can be seen entering the Kicking Horse Valley from the left side of the panorama. The panorama also includes one of the best views of the colossal crags that guard the upper valley. Cathedral Mountain is a towering giant, one of the more impressive mountains in the area. The highway and the railway pass directly below it. From the highway you have to crane your neck upward to see its summit wreathed in curling mist.

In 1980 a portion of Yoho National park was set aside by a United Nations decree as a World Heritage Site. At first glance it is easy to see what might have attracted international attention to the park. It was not the peaks themselves, however, that warranted such prestigious designation. Far up the shoulder of Wapta Peak, Dr. Charles Walcott, Secretary of the Smithsonian Institution, found beds of ancient fossils revealing the best preserved examples of life in this planet's earliest seas. In 1909 Walcott was hiking the highline trail above Emerald Lake when he found a shattered fossil form that greatly interested him. He found others on the slope above it, and eventually discovered a major outcrop rich in fossilized life forms that existed 600 million years ago, when an ancient sea occupied the site of these mountains. Excavations from 1910 to 1916 revealed the size and importance of the find. A second site was discovered on the very steep slopes of Mt. Stephen. Strata containing the poisonous sink hole where Cambrian creatures perished, surfaced on the side of the mountain. The sites were excavated again and again, as paleontologists pieced together increasingly complex pictures of life on earth when the first sediments were being laid down to form these mountains.

Another pleasant surprise in Yoho National Park is the little town of Field. This unassuming clutter of clapboard houses and tiny shops possesses the pleasant ambience that attracted turn of the century visitors to Banff and Lake Louise. Only two hundred people live in the park year round, but Field has a surprising abundance of characters who wear their years of mountain experience comfortably, like they might a well-worn hiking coat. Despite the remoteness and the weathered look of the town, the locals are not backcountry hicks. Many are extremely well read. Some even publish their own books. Many travel a great deal. Some collect fine paintings of the mountain country they love, and a surprising number of them take their wine seriously, savouring good vintages from all around the world. There is a retired warden who displays his rock collection in the sun room of his house. In springtime he will take a few friends to hidden glades in the greening valley to find rare orchids and stones of a thousand hues. His wife studied art with members of the Group Of Seven when they taught at the art school in Banff. With a glass of whiskey in hand, he can summarize a century of mountaineering rescues, give the dates of horse trips into remote valleys, and remember a hundred old timers who worked for the railway during the steam age. Some of the people who live in the town were born there and have stayed. Despite the harsh winters and the dangerous roads, they prefer their close proximity to huge peaks. In few other places in the Rockies do avalanches rumble into the backstreets of town. Nowhere else do so many elk wander the night streets. The summer staff who come from the east to work in the campgrounds and the tourist information centres are often a little afraid of the place. The wildness comes right into town. At most they stay a couple of years and move on to where it's brighter in winter and the blizzards don't last so long. They leave behind the old core of the town, the survivors who still feel a deep sense of wonder toward their mountains.

Crowfoot Glacier

Bow Peak (2868 m)

Mt. Jimmy Simpson (3012 m)

Mt. Thompson (3065 m)

Num-ti-jah Lodge

Bow Lake

BOW LAKE   09:00

The exposure was chosen to emphasize the vertical bands of colour in the lake. To add dimension to the rock face directly across the lake, the early morning light proved best for this scene. Ultraviolet light levels in this area pose a problem for exposure and colour saturation. An 81A correction filter was chosen to give more accurate colours. None of the panoramas in this book were taken with a polarizing filter as it would render the sky an odd colour.

Portal Peak (2790 m)

Bow Glacier

Crowfoot Mtn. (3050 m)

BOW LAKE

AND JIMMY SIMPSON'S LODGE

Pilgrims To Various Peaks

One of the extreme pleasures of travelling in the mountain national parks in Canada is the sheer sense of aloneness that accompanies every step one takes into the backcountry. Part of this joy of exploration is founded upon the fact that the land has not changed significantly since men first wandered into these valleys looking not for silence, but simply for a way through them. Here it is very easy to feel as if you are the first to make your way into the high country. In this sense, the landscape experience becomes extremely personal. In a brief day's walk the mountains and their various weathers and life patterns become a brief but intimate part of one's own life. Though several people might take a single journey together, the number of experiences will be as varied as the individuals who take part. One might remember the conversation, the steep trails or lunch on bright meadows. Another will be reminded of the introspective sense of the self that often overcomes people in the dwarfing presence of big mountains. Occasionally, something even stranger happens. When one is too tired to impose urban values onto the surrounding landscape, when one is too exhausted to banter the usual superficialities in conversation, when at last we are reduced to our elemental selves, a subtle surrender may take place in which we may come as close as possible to an understanding of the raw wildness of the earth.

We wear our cultures like clothes. Sometimes stripped naked, we are confronted by brutal, humbling new realizations. When this occurs the experience is often accompanied by hardship and even some danger. Only by competently experiencing such nakedness again and again can one come to accept this state without fear. There may even come a point where you might find yourself genuinely accepting the awkward frailty humans bring to summits of every kind. In this acceptance is a remarkable peace. Suddenly one can admit to the conceit of ambition, the utter futility, and collective idiocy that are inherently part of every culture. This knowledge affords grace, and those who have known it usually make their way back to the valleys with a light step. They seem to possess a unique perspective and a folk wisdom that makes them interesting to others. Pilgrims tend to find their way to such summiteers, seeking direction to their own various peaks. The history of the Rockies is rich in such characters, and among the foremost of these was the man who built the lodge on the edge of the lake in this panorama.

Black Sheep, Wild Sheep and Bighorn Rams

James Justin McCartney Simpson was born in Stamford, England on August 8, 1877. He was a spirited child capable of a broad range of mischief. Although he came from an upstanding family, young James did not appear to have much respect for authority. This was evident in his poaching activities on the estate of the Marquis of Exeter and in a certain little indiscretion he committed one day in the church the family attended. It appears an unseemly affair had been discovered involving the Reverend, and the good minister had been relieved of his post. Young Jim was in uncomfortable attendance on the day of the minister's final sermon. Upon taking final leave of the congregation, the Reverend walked slowly down the aisle, a sprig of mistletoe attached at belt level to the back of his vestment. Quite contrary to good Victorian manners, Jim not only noticed the mistletoe but in loud guffaw brought the attention of the entire congregation to the minister's subtle revenge. This was too much for his family, and they reacted as many upstanding Brits of the period did toward a disgraceful child. They sent him to the colonies.

In 1896 Simpson arrived in Canada with express instructions to take up legitimate work in Manitoba. He spent one March night on a farm near Winnipeg and concluded that such a harsh life was decidedly not for him. He retired to the city for precisely the length of time it took for him to drink away the money his family sent with him. By way of escape, he stowed away on a westbound train only to be thrown off by a conductor at Silver City. He walked to Laggan, near Lake Louise. Propitiously, it was in the mountains, and not on the lonely plains, that Simpson was heaved from the train.

In Laggan, Simpson had to find work if he was going to survive. Jim was forced to sully his gentlemanly reputation by working with pick and shovel on a railway maintenance gang. Typical of many seasonal Banff residents after a summer of hard work, Jim left for warmer climes. His money ran out in San Francisco where he later found himself involved in a political march, planning to cross the entire U.S. to Washington. Unclear as to the motives of the demonstration, Simpson fell out with the group when it reached New Mexico, and took another railway job until he could afford to go west again to Los Angeles. After working on a sealing ship for a time, he remembered an offer made by outfitter Tom Wilson during the summer he spent in Banff. Wilson had appreciated Simpson's style and suggested he could come work for his outfit anytime he liked. Simpson returned to the Rockies, and a legacy began.

The Camp Cook Makes Good

Being junior in the outfit when he came to work for Tom Wilson in the summer of 1897, Simpson was assigned the job of camp cook. In his first year he met many of Wilson's most important and influential clients. At a camp at Emerald Lake he entertained William, George, and Mary Vaux who had been recently involved in glaciological studies in the Rogers Pass area. He also met Dr. Charles Schäffer and his young wife Mary, a women who would, in time, leave her own mark on the history of the Rockies.

One of the most interesting parties Simpson was involved with in his brief but highly celebrated career as camp cook was the Walling expedition to Mt. Assiniboine. The brothers, Willoughby and English Walling, were the first to use Swiss mountain guides in an attempt to climb this major mountain. Jimmy Simpson recalled the affair as something of a disaster. After an unsuccessful attempt on the peak the climbers and their guides took the Spray River route back to Banff, while Simpson and the pack train followed the traditional path over Whiteman's Pass to Canmore. The Swiss guides, apparently disgusted with the Wallings' incompetence, abandoned them near Banff. Within fifty meters of a logging road leading to the Banff Springs Hotel, the brothers, certain they were lost for good, killed a horse to fend off starvation. When Tom Wilson heard the details of their disastrous trip, he offered them a free week on the trail in the Lake Louise area. Simpson cooked on this outfit too. It was one of many hunting trips Simpson would enjoy in the regions of the upper Bow River.

Jimmy Simpson also spent a day with the famous Edward Whymper, conqueror of the Matterhorn, easily the most famous mountaineer in all the Victorian world. Whymper was in the Rockies promoting mountaineering for the Canadian Pacific Railway. Although he was a heavy drinker past his climbing prime, he cut a wide swath at his camp in the Yoho Valley. In Ted Hart's magical *Diamond Hitch,* a chronicle of the first packers and guides, Jim Simpson remembers that day he spent drinking with Whymper in Field, B.C. It is easy to imagine the two hitting it right off:

> "Whymper was peculiar, possibly because he had been lionized too much, but he was so determined an individual and such a strong character that he resembled a bulldog very much like the cartoons of that dog standing astride the Union Jack ready to devour anyone who touched it . . . He got me very drunk at the old Field Hotel after the camp was over and confided he had a very clever brother who drank himself to death and said he, "Yes Simpson, very clever and I often used to say to him 'George, why don't you take it in moderation the same as I do." You know what moderation he used . . ."

Wolverine Go Quickly

By 1901, Simpson was well ensconced in the Rockies. A developing reputation and good connections ensured him of a long career, and he was anxious to take full advantage of the opportunity the new land offered. In the winter following Whymper's visit to the Rockies, Simpson and fellow packer Fred Ballard began trapping in the huge expanse of country extending from Bow Lake to the Alexandra River. It was during this period Simpson developed his legendary skills on snowshoes and a reputation for fierce defense of the cabins that dotted his long trapline.

The great variations in temperature, common during most winters in the Rockies, decreed that snow conditions could change dramatically during storms, or when chinook winds blew warmly from the Pacific. As it took several days to traverse the trapline even in good conditions, it was essential the trapper be highly skilled in winter travel. Simpson earned the name "Nashan-esen" from the Stoney Indians. The name means "wolverine-go-quickly", an honourable appellation not shared by Simpson's partner Fred Ballard who was less able at the use of snowshoes. Simpson recalled the day Ballard was following in his tracks wearing a pair of oil-tanned shoepacks which were used when there was little snow. Ballard caught an edge on a pine pole and created what he called a "buffalo waller" in the snow. The air turned blue with Ballard's rage, and Simpson hurried to the cabin leaving his partner alone to cool down. Still livid upon his arrival, Ballard threw the shoepacks down and pointed his loaded rifle at them, defying them to move. Fortunately, they remained still and were spared another day.

As early trappers often travelled in extreme conditions, their small, well stocked cabins were essential to their survival while on the line. It was critical the cabins not be looted in the trappers absence. Simpson and Ballard took security in these back-country refuges seriously, indeed. Often doors and windows were booby trapped, and notices on the cabin doors warned intruders of the risk they were taking by breaking into a Simpson cabin. Sometimes the warnings were in poetic form. The following was found on a slab of wood on the door of Simpson's trapline cabin in the Mistaya River Valley:

These few lines are dedicated to the low lived sucker
who is in the habit of breaking in here.

If you look for excitement, be ye here
When the owner hereof is standing near.
Proceed at the game of breaking in,
But mutter farewell to all your kin.

You son of a gun(?), you've not the nerve
To let the owner of this observe
The way in which the deed is done
Or, Jesus Christ, we'd have some fun.

Num-Ti-Jah Lodge

The next era in Jimmy Simpson's life was fashioned, oddly enough, by the introduction of a new technology to the Rocky Mountains. When the first automobiles came west there was great fear among outfitters and guides that roads would ultimately find their way into every valley and to the summit of every accessible pass. The rising numbers of tourists that would come in the wake of this development would not be interested in travelling by horse. Outfitting would come to an end and the mountains would no longer be pleasant to live in. Organized opposition to automobiles in the national parks could not stem enthusiasm for this new means of travel. Soon the outfitting community was looking for ways to take advantage of the encroaching technology that was bound to change the Rockies for good.

It was apparent Jimmy Simpson was looking for a place to settle down. He'd already picked the location for the lodge he talked of building since his first visit to Bow Lake with Bill Peyto in 1895. Since a large hotel in the railway tradition was out of the question, he chose a single lodge he might use as a centre for his outfitting operations in the upper Bow Valley, an area he knew well from his trapping years.

In 1920 Simpson applied to the Parks Branch for the lease of five acres on the shores of Bow Lake, one of his favourite camping spots. Parks officials notified him that he could only be granted the lease with the proviso that five thousand dollars worth of improvements be made to the site. Using the stunted trees at the high altitude of Bow Lake, Simpson designed and built an octagonal building with sides no longer than ten feet. Windows and doors, required to finish the interior, were hauled by horse from

Laggan. He named the lodge "Num-Ti-Jah", the Indian name for pine marten, an animal he had trapped abundantly along his early lines. The building was not completed until 1922, and it wasn't until a year later that Simpson was able to entertain his first paying guests, the distinguished mountaineers J. Monroe Thorington and William S. Ladd, who were en route to climbs in the Columbia Icefield area.

It took almost two decades for Simpson's prediction to fulfill itself; that automobiles would change the nature of tourism in the Rockies. During the Great Depression of the 1930s, relief workers constructed the Banff-Jasper Highway. When it was officially opened in 1940, Num-Ti-Jah was one of only two lodges along the entire route. Rightly anticipating increased visitation along the completed highway, Simpson initiated construction of a second, larger lodge on the site in 1937. It is this building that has the famous red roof so visible at the edge of the lake in the panorama. When the new lodge was completed, Jimmy turned the first lodge into a personal retreat. Filled with many treasures from his early years as an outfitter and hunting guide, this is one of the most historic buildings remaining in the Rockies.

Jimmy Simpson gradually acquired the status of Grand Old Man of the Mountains, as he aged gracefully in the famous retreat he built for himself at Bow Lake. During the time he ran Num-Ti-Jah, he entertained most of the important historical figures passing through on their way to climb summits of the famous mountains of that era of Canadian history. Though he passed the operational reins of his business to his son during the 1940s, he remained an important part of the living history of the area until his death in 1972, at the ripe age of ninety-five. Right up until he died, pilgrims came to hear his stories and to bask in the wisdom of his decades among wilderness peaks.

eyto Peak (2970 m)

Mt. Baker (3172 m)

Mt. Jimmy Simpson (3012 m)

084 m)

Mt. Patterson (3197 m)

Mt. Murchison (3333 m)

Mt. Wilson (3260 m)

PEYTO LAKE   06:30

It is possible to use wide angle lenses to represent a view, however the horizon will tend to "squash" from the distortion of a wide angle lens. This scene is ideal panorama material. The lake is fed by a glacier which flows to an outwash then to the lake itself and finally drains into a valley. The complete scene is in one exposure without distortion. Cold air rests like a blanket on the surface of the water and holds the water calm.

Peyto Lake

Silverhorn Mtn. (2910 m)

Mt. Weed (3080 m)

M

PEYTO LAKE

AND THE MISTAYA VALLEY

An Assertive Blue

There are few places in the Canadian Rockies that have more immediate impact on the visitor than Peyto Lake. The view is from a lookout above the crest of Bow Summit on the Icefield Parkway. To the left is Peyto Peak (pronounced Pee-toe), named for Bill Peyto, a notorious local guide who first brought visitors to the lake in the summer of 1895. Beyond and right of the peak is the Wapta Icefield, an eighty square kilometre névé that straddles the Great Divide between Banff and Yoho National Parks. Out of this high basin tumble a dozen or so small and large glaciers. The Peyto Glacier can be seen flowing into inky morning shadow. Melt from this glacier and snow that falls on it has created an enormous outwash where tonnes of silt and rock flour are dumped as the water meanders toward the basin of the lake. The opaque blue of the water is created by light refracting through the fine particles of suspended silt.

The view presents itself after a short walk that terminates at a man-made platform. To avoid the heat haze that often appears on hot summer days, the panorama was taken just after dawn. By noon on a clear day, the colour of the water can be so bright it rivals the blue of the most perfect sky. But even pictures cannot prepare you for it. Suddenly, you find yourself suspended more than three hundred metres above the unnaturally blue water of the exquisite lake. The valley is called Mistaya, an Indian word for grizzly bear, an animal still encountered in this part of the park. The mountain dominating the view is Mt. Patterson. A cleft in this mountain cradles a magnificent glacier which travellers can stop to admire from the highway that winds through the valley. The Snowbird Glacier clings to steep cliff bands on the mountain's northeast face and is shaped like a great white bird frozen in graceful descent from a high and windy sky. Blue-throated crevasses in the ice are the same colour as Peyto Lake. Over a hundred other glaciers are visible from the

Icefield Parkway, as it gracefully winds through the valley floor from Lake Louise to Jasper townsite.

A Lake The Colour Of Bill Peyto's Eyes

It is appropriate that the lake, the peak, and the glacier are all named for a famous local outfitter. When the Rockies were first explored and mapped, guides and horse packers played an essential role in route-finding and trail-making, often in survival threatening situations in remote forests. Many of the horse packers came with the first surveys of the rail route. When the track was laid they stayed on because they liked the country, or because they could see opportunity in the developing tourism trade that came riding in on the trains. Four remarkable characters emerged from the rough and often unruly outfitters of the early railway era. Tom Wilson outfitted for A. B. Rogers, the crude American utterly committed to finding a feasible route for the Canadian Pacific Railway through the Selkirk Mountains in central British Columbia. It was Wilson who was led by an Indian companion to the shores of Lake Louise. Jimmy Simpson, the black sheep son of a British aristocrat, hired on with Tom Wilson as a packer, but later became famous for the lodge he built at Bow Lake, just below the Peyto viewpoint.

Jim Brewster began guiding a decade after packing became popular in Banff by connecting himself with the Banff Springs Hotel. He free-wheeled his guiding company into a huge tour operation he called Brewster Transport. To keep abreast of trends in transportation, he introduced cars, then buses to the Rockies. Brewster buses can still be seen parked near the viewpoint where this panorama was taken.

Bill Peyto came to the Banff area in 1887. After a stint on the railroad, he worked as an apprentice guide with Tom Wilson. He, too, was a bona fide character who became a legend in Banff. In winter, he took up trapping in the Sunshine Village area of Banff National Park. Alone, he haunted his trapline for weeks on end, staying in a series of log cabins he constructed along the line. Peyto cut a dashing, romantic figure. He was famous for his wide brimmed hat, wild blue eyes, and a long moustache that made him vaguely desperado-like in appearance. Though he often wore a sidearm, his attire was not complete unless he wore a white kerchief that looked surprisingly like a linen napkin stolen from the Banff Springs Hotel. If Peyto's appearance was not enough to inspire a legend, surely his actions would qualify him for any Mountain Man Hall of Fame. While on his own in the backcountry, he devised some amusing practical jokes which he played on his friends during his rare visits to town. The day he showed up in Banff with a live lynx strapped to his back was one of his best. The patrons of the Cascade Hotel tavern showed much interest in Peyto's snarling companion and were suitably aghast when he released it in the bar.

Men like Bill Peyto made it possible for visiting American and British mountaineers to access the unclimbed peaks of the Rockies. Though their outfitting skills were often highly regarded by these climbers, their importance was usually forgotten in the storytelling and legend-making that followed the famous first ascents of major peaks. It should be noted, however, that when the climbers went home to be fêted for their accomplishments, outfitters like Bill Peyto stayed to build and improve trails into the wilderness for future generations of romantics who came to the Rockies to drink in the silence and the beauty. It is to men like Bill Peyto that we owe our easy access to the high places.

A Grinding and Suffering Of Stone

From Bow Summit even the most casual viewer has to notice the extent to which the valley has been sculpted into pleasing visual forms. From the Peyto Lake viewpoint a motorist can be confronted by all the major features that compose the rock-tumble of alpine ecology in the Rockies. The panorama format reveals the entire vista at a glance. Two major influences are responsible for the existence of the valley and its roughly hewn peaks. The first, mountain building, is a complex and slowly unfolding process about which little is known. The second process, glaciation, is fast-acting compared to mountain building. Evidence of glacial dynamics can be seen directly and indirectly everywhere in the valley.

The Canadian Rockies are young mountains, at least in terms of geological time. Though the Rockies have only been in existence for about one hundred and twenty-five million years, the rocks that compose them are much older. It is hard to clearly define when the process of their evolution began, but it is evident that sediments forming in an inland ocean six hundred million years ago, eventually hardened into the strata of these peaks. Apparently, the central part of the North American continent was also depressed. An enormous basin extended from western Manitoba across the prairies to eastern British Columbia. A warm, shallow tongue of the Pacific Ocean filled this trough, and into it poured sediments and debris carried by rivers that eroded surrounding landscapes. Though the sea came and went over hundreds of millions of years, the sediments grew deeper and deeper as the trough settled under the amassing weight. The accumulation reached depths of up to sixteen kilometres, creating pressures and temperatures that hardened sediments into stone. About one hundred and twenty-five million years ago, a collision between great crustal plates carrying the earth's continents caused central North America to rise from the floor of the sea. In western North America, where the influence of the collision was greatest, the sea floor jumbled and fractured into mountains.

At Peyto viewpoint the sedimentary nature of the Rockies is very obvious. The gently dipping strata of Mt. Patterson have accumulated on Cambrian quartzites that compose the lower part of the mountain. These quartzites reveal the oceanic beginnings of the Rockies. If you could cross the raging torrent of the Mistaya River to reach the mountain, you might find fossil evidence of the creatures that wriggled in that ancient sea. Certainly fossils are common in this valley. From them, scientists have learned much about the evolution of marine life in the ancient past. By comparing these fossils to those found in other regions of the world, it has become possible to surmise what conditions of existence might have been like on this planet more than six hundred million years ago. The strata are like pages in a book, each chapter bound together by some catastrophe, some global disaster that caused the nature of what the rivers carried to that forgotten sea to change utterly. But the pages are not all in order. The library has been looted by time, and the books are all on end.

As the Rockies rose they looked little as they do now. Their orogeny was slow; a painful grinding and suffering of stone. Even as they were rising, wind and water were shaping them. Rivers ran deeply into fractures, penetrating the very roots of the peaks. Forests obscured the rising summits. Trees and the first grasses groped thirstily over the stone. Separated from one another by deep river valleys, the mountains grew rounded and worn. The rock of sediments is soft. Unlike granite and other forms of the cooling earth's crust, an old seafloor will dissolve in the wind. It will wear quickly away, as if the stone were poised eager to leap into a new form.

Winter For Forty Thousand Years

It is hard to reckon how often ice has careened across the cooling surface of the earth. Though the evidence of one is usually erased by the next, the skid marks of at least four glacial advances can be found. Glaciations might be tied to some interplanetary cause, perhaps to comets and the impact of their nuclear collisions with the earth. If this were so, surely craters would disclose such a past. Perhaps the sun cools and warms, a thermostat of uncertain stellar means. Maybe the atmosphere changes or is altered by volcanoes or the whims of shortsighted inhabitants tampering with time. For whatever reason, the advancing ice brings change. In these mountains, it created wide valleys and peaks carved into stone arrows pointing.

The last major North American glaciation began fifty thousand years ago. The climate cooled and snow fell around the Arctic Circle. It fell on cold summits and high valleys pushed skyward by the slow rise of the peaks. Glaciology offers us clear evidence of a terrifying fact. The seasons do not always follow known schedules. Doubtful if anyone noticed, one year the spring did not come. Snow fell but didn't melt. Instead, it accumulated like sediments and, compressed by its own thickening mass, became ice. Then the ice began to move. South, east and westward from the spine of the Rockies, it ground and scraped the earth. It is cold comfort to know winter can last for forty thousand years.

Only theories can explain why the climate changed again and the earth warmed. The ice dissolved into unimaginable torrents as glaciers retreated to the north and back up into the high places from whence they came. The absent ice revealed a landscape changed. What were once steep but gently smoothed and forested mountains became naked, jagged peaks. The entire landscape was torn apart and mired in its own debris. There was desolation everywhere; no sound pierced the thunder of great rivers pouring out onto the plains.

From Peyto viewpoint, the visitor can witness the last vestige of retreating ice. The big glacier is still there. So is the icefield that formed it. Every summer meltwater rumbles through the valley. The lake turns an assertive blue with the debris the ice yields. The forest has returned. Tentatively, at first, it followed the melting ice into the valleys, but now the trees march boldly toward the peaks. But the scene is beguiling. This is only an intermission. The ice is waiting. Waiting.

Mt. Andromeda (3450 m)

Nigel Peak (3211 m)

Mt. Wilcox (2884 m)

PARKER RIDGE   11:30

High alpine meadows are beautiful places to be on a warm day. Although this area is not a long hike, it becomes difficult with 45 pounds of equipment. This meadow is on the edge of the tree line with superb views in all directions. Late morning light seemed to be the best choice.

Cirrus Mtn. (3270 m)

Mt. Athabasca (3491 m)

Mt. Hilda (3060 m)

PARKER RIDGE

AND THE ATHABASCA MASSIF

The Ultimate Alpine

There are only two places on the Icefield Parkway where the highway reaches up into the high alpine. At Bow Summit and at Sunwapta Pass you can drive to the edge of treeline and cross into the alpine, the most hostile of all the life zones in the Rockies. Though the arctic may be colder, only the earth's poles experience greater extremes of temperature, more frequent frosts, and shorter seasons of growth. In this panorama, the viewer is introduced to the entire range of alpine influences that shape all landscapes above timberline in all the world's high mountains.

A few thousand years ago this area was buried completely beneath ice. The ice has retreated from most of North America except where heavy snowfall, altitude, and short summers combine to invite the last ice age to linger in high basins along the Continental Divide. Here the ice continues to sculpt the land and remains potent evidence of how dramatically climates could change and how rapidly glaciers can advance again over unsuspecting terrain. The very shape of the landscape has been determined by active ice. The great peak of Mt. Athabasca was carved by three glaciers gnawing simultaneously into the massif of gradually yielding stone. The glaciers gouged through weakening ridges, forming a ring of ice around the impressive Matterhorn-like spire.

First Soil

When the mountain-shaped glaciers melted, they deposited boulders they once carried within them. The retreating ice also left behind a thin layer of gravel, called till, and a poor, bankrupt soil. Life forms itself in this frail medium and struggles upwards toward the peaks. The process is gradual, indeed. On the prairies to the east, one hundred years have passed for every three centimetres of soil created, about one century for every inch. At Parker Ridge, in Banff

National Park, it takes a lot longer for soils to grow. Time seems anaesthetised by the cold. In a century only a skiff of soil has formed on the crumbling stone. Even as the soil increases and plants take hold, all the bitter influences of the high altitude are in league against it.

Snow cover is a relentless enemy of stabilizing plants. Beneath the snow, the tundra soil is thin and easily saturated. Thawing soil simply cannot accommodate moisture released from melt. On steep slopes gravity pulls moisture-saturated soil downhill, carrying with it rooted plant communities. Whole slopes and entire rafts of plants creep steadily downward. Developing flowers drown in mud, and whole slopes become exposed to the further action of cold and wind. In advanced stages this process, called soli-fluction, can only be stopped by bedrock outcrops and particularly well-rooted communities of plants. To survive in the high alpine, plants must adjust to the moving rafts of soil. Miraculously, they do just that.

Frost Blows The Rocks Apart

The water of melt and rain is life-giving to the plants of the high tundra; sometimes it also kills. In the cold night, the rock of the mountains cools and contracts. Water trapped in cracks and fissures in the rock quickly freezes and expands. The pressure of expanding ice can reach seven tons per square inch, the same force you might expect to get by dropping a truck on something the size of a marble. Big rocks explode into little rocks; plants containing too much moisture are blown apart by the cold. In a high, cold place at treeline, the number of frost-free days each year is few. In many places in the Rockies, rarely a week goes by, even in mid-summer, when it doesn't freeze. Plants respond to the threat of cold by huddling together to create micro-climates of pocketed warmth by which one plant will protect the next from wind and advancing cold night air. They cover themselves with tiny hairs to insulate their soft moist tissues. They shape their flowers like deep dishes to reflect the warmth toward to the developing flower, and they coat their precious petals with wax to prevent the wind from stealing the moisture so carefully gleaned from the thin soil The alpine is an ecology of slender means; the kind of plant community where it is easy to respect the survivors just for their tenacity and bold pluck in standing up (or laying down) against the ruthless violence of the high heavens themselves.

An Unlikely Marriage Endures

Lichens, very simple plants, are usually the first living things to cultivate the bare rock of the post-glacial moonscape. Even the casual traveller at timberline can spot them clinging to boulders and exposed stones on south-facing cliffs. Lichens are remarkable organisms. They are two plants, really, married by form and function to permit them to overcome the most hostile conditions plants can face on the planet. The marriage is an unlikely one. Rock lichens are pioneers. They are common in the most disagreeable landscapes and receive the least attention from photographers and other aficionados of life on the extreme edge. A primitive fungus attaches itself to the rock and absorbs nutrients from the air, or from slowly dissolving minerals in the rock. There are few nutrients the fungus can capture, but what it is able to garner, it passes on to the algae with which it co-exists. This algae is capable of limited amounts of photosynthesis by which it processes the nutrient material into useable plant food. In exchange for the supply of raw materials, the algae passes processed food back to the fungus. Both are able to survive by their co-operative energy agreement developed over millions of years in the most hostile territory. A by-product of this union is humic acid, the forerunner of humis, one of the central elements of all fertile soil. It is in the build-up of humis produced by lichens that allows complex life forms to cultivate and take root as their seeds fall on the thin, virgin ground above treeline. The process, however, is very, very slow. Rhizocarpon geographicum, or map lichen, as it is called for its mottled green and black map-like appearance, is a good example of the slow metabolic process of pioneer vegetation in the cold of the alpine. It grows at the outrageous rate of about a centimeter every thousand years. Its growth rate is so predictable that it has been used as an archaeological dating device. If you find a lichen-covered stone hammer, you might be able to guess how long ago it was made.

The Solar Wind

Even on the high saddle of Parker Ridge, where a lichen colony has spent a few millennium cultivating the soil, more complex plants are not guaranteed a strong foothold. After soil and moisture, wind is the next big factor in determining survival on the boundary between the forest and the sky. Wind carries away fine soil as it forms. The air, in continual motion, cools the earth's surface and dries the leaves of the plants that hug it. Wind blows the winter snow away and claws at exposed parts of plants. At the upward limit of plant growth, the wind can be fierce. Above timberline the world turns continually through the clear, icy air of the high atmosphere. Dwarfism is the only way to survive. Because the plants of the tundra are short, they do whatever they can to stay out of the wind. There is a second kind of wind that blows wildly over the summits of the high ridges. It is the sun's wind, the fierce solar rays that bombard the plants and animals of the alpine with ultraviolet radiation. This wind accounts for the brightness of the colours of the flowers and for fierce sunburn to alpine travellers.

The first plants to occupy the barrens above timberline are cushion-like, composed of tiny florets that feel their way slowly outward from a small centre and make their way from soil patch to soil patch as their slowly growing roots permit. The moss campion is one of these plants. The growing season above timberline can be very short, for the tundra warms only briefly before the shortening days rob the soil of heat. Plants grow slowly. The moss campion is one of the heartiest of the alpine plants. In twenty years it will produce a flower; in twenty-five years it may reach a hands-breadth across. The incredible success of the moss campion as a pioneer can be measured by the number of grasses and flowering plants that take root in the campion's sheltered centre. In the warmth of its central leaves, other plants develop and disperse, changing gradually the face of the tundra. Sedges and grasses eventually take over, creating high meadows. It was from the edge of such a meadow this panorama was taken.

Reproduction in plants is also a serious problem at extreme altitudes in the Rockies. Insects most frequently bear the pollen for tundra flowers. During the brief summer, Parker Ridge buzzes with millions of flying creatures making their specialized way among the flowers. The buttercup attracts flies, while the larkspur attracts only bees. Pollination is not usually a problem unless the summer season is unusually short or abnormally cold. Where competition for the thin soil is fierce, it will die. Good real estate is in demand

even at the highest places on earth.

One way plants ensure propagation in an advantageous environment is by planting the seed themselves. At least two plants in the tundra do just that. The wild strawberry sends vegetative runners along the ground's surface to find water and deep soil. If they find warm hollows and adequate moisture, they root and form new plants. It can also disperse by ordinary means, forming seeds into a luscious berry designed to be eaten, or to fall ripened from the stem. The mountain bistort uses another technique to ensure propogation. It develops seedlings on its own stalk, nurturing them until they mature. The seedlings then drop in a ring around the mother plant and, sheltered by it, grow in the developed soil.

For all the incredible adaptive capabilities of high alpine plants, they are incapable of adapting to one major thing. Though they withstand deep cold, wind, short summers, and drought, they don't survive compression. If you walk on alpine plants, especially in the fall or winter when they are most vulnerable, they die. If you drop something on them they perish. Litter at high altitudes takes a long time to decompose. A cigarette package on the meadow shields light from the plants below; it disturbs the microclimate plants create around themselves to survive. A soft drink tin can smother what took a century to grow. People are new to the alpine. Tundra plants cannot adapt to us. If we travel here, we must adapt to them.

The High Desert

In a land where each ecology is fashioned by cold, it is odd that heat is also a problem. In many ways the summit of Sunwapta Pass is a high desert. In the warm days of July and August the sun, though warming developing flowers, robs the soil of moisture. Rainfall is at a premium during these months before the onset of prolonged frost in September. Whereas in the spring too much water melts into the thin soppy soil, the problem now is drought. Despite drought, alpine plants use the long dry days of late summer to mature their seeds. These are critical days. The amount of energy stored in developing seeds determines how next year's flowers will do against the cold. If the season is long and the flower matures strong, vital seeds, the anemone, for example, will flower vigorously the next spring despite inclement weather. The flower may burst right through the snow and still thrive.

The trees waiting on the upper edge of the forest have seen the tundra flowers gather together for warmth and resistance to the wind. They have watched the creation of separate weathers and new techniques for survival against deep snow, frost, and wind. The fir trees advance upward too, by tunneling. Roots making their way silently beneath the shallow earth do not expose themselves to fierce winds, frost, or sun. By sprouting living offspring around the mother plant, fir trees are able to tunnel toward the summits. When winter snows push the lower branches of these trees into the ground, they take root. In time the rooted branches become mature firs, each clustering around a soil-hollow the mother tree created as it adapted to the prevailing wind. These clusters of crooked, wind-torn trees are called krumholz. Deep within the shelter of their dense, dry branches, it can be calm enough to read, even in the wildest lightning and rain storm.

Animals in the high tundra are comparatively rare. Columbian ground squirrels burrow into the deeper soil at treeline. Occasionally, moose will follow the willows up out of the valleys to where these bushes shrink to the ground before the ceaseless wind. Hoary marmots whistle from sun warmed rocks in summer. Tail-less hares called pikas do not hibernate and can occasionally be found in tunnels beneath the snow. The ptarmigan, a species of high altitude grouse, inhabits the tundra all year round. Goats often come down from the peaks to feed in the lush meadows above timberline. Bighorn sheep gather in small herds between wind-flagged stands of gnarled fir. Black bears can be found in the berry bushes. The grizzly bear is also an inhabitat

of this high region. It feeds on rodents, the choice roots of certain flowering plants, and on carcasses of mountain sheep and goats. In the almost alien clearness of high mountain light, all things are married to the cold, short seasons of life.

Mt. Andromeda (3450 m)

Mt. Athabasca (3491 m)

Columbia Icefield Chalet

The Icefields Park

THE COLUMBIA ICEFIELD   10:45

After many trips to this location, I was always looking for a better way for the lodge to be represented. After searching many possible sites, I found this location and the tree added the element I had been looking for. The wind twists these trees on exposed slopes into various shapes.

Mount Wilcox (2884 m)

Mt. Kitchener (3480 m)

Snow Dome (3451 m)

Dome Glacier

Athbasca Glacier

way

THE COLUMBIA ICEFIELD

The Snows of Yesteryear

The Columbia Icefield straddles the Great Divide and the border between Banff and Jasper National Parks. It is an immense natural feature, thickly blanketing more than three hundred square kilometres of the high peaks and valleys along the Great Divide. Even from an airplane it is difficult to see it all at once. From the Icefield Parkway one can glimpse it a glacier at a time. Nevertheless, the highway approach to the Athabasca Glacier is an awesome experience. It is the only place in the Rockies, and one of the few places in the world, where you can drive right to the toe of a major glacier, get out of your car, and touch ice that may have fallen as snow while Jacques Cartier was sighting the eastern coast of Canada, four hundred years ago.

Even the most casual observer will notice that glacial ice has had major impact on most Canadian landscapes. Ice smoothed and accentuated the northern tundra and completely flattened the western plains. The bleak and ancient rock of the Canadian Shield was scoured by each successful advance of ice. The mountains have been gouged and ripped apart in a cold history of rumbling, grinding glaciers. There are a few places, in the south and along each coast, that have escaped the terrible abrasion. Despite the massive influence that glaciers have had in shaping Canada, very little is known about how glaciers are created and why they behave as they do. Certainly we know their origin and growth are tied to macro-climatic changes that have influenced the way man has come to inhabit this planet. Weather cools, rain falls and turns to snow. Snow is compressed by weight and time into ice. Glaciers grow and advance. Oceans shrink as more and more of the earth's water is bound in ice. We know these patterns can reverse quickly, causing rapid, dramatic melt. We know also that glaciers are affected by local micro-climatic changes and can influence the very conditions that sustain them. In some terrifying way, glaciers are capable of creating their own weather. Once begun, there is nothing we can do to stop their blind advance.

Remaining glacial masses often form important watersheds. The Columbia Icefield is the source of three of the greatest river systems in North America. If one could dump a bucket of water over the summit of Snow Dome, its contents would splash onto the waiting ice, then find its way into three different rivers. From this rare triple continental divide, water flows north through the Athabasca River system, into the Mackenzie, and the Arctic Ocean. Water flowing south and east from the divide enters the North Saskatchewan River, and the Atlantic Ocean at Hudson's Bay. Water flowing westward from the divide joins the Columbia River, then enters the Pacific near Portland, Oregon.

In Search Of Cold Giants

Professor A. P. Coleman, a geologist with the University of Toronto, first came to the Rockies answering the call of the Canadian Pacific Railway which touted its system as the easy and safe way to visit "The Canadian Alps". He rode to tracks' end at Laggan in 1884 and to the Selkirk Mountains west of the Rockies in 1885. At that time there was a controversy raging about the height of the highest mountains in the area of the Great Divide. The early maps of David Thompson, and subsequent observations by the botanist David Douglas, had cited the summit of Athabasca Pass at more than 11,000 feet. If this were true, the peaks on either side of the pass, Mount Hooker and Brown, were held to be 15,000 feet or more, giants of more than 4000 metres in height. In 1888 Coleman returned to the Rockies with a young companion, Frank Stover, to look for these mountains. They went home disappointed however, unable to complete the journey up the tree-tangled

and swollen Columbia River. Coleman resumed the search in 1892, approaching the mountain from the foothills to the east. From a mountain top near the forks of the Brazeau River, Coleman searched the horizon for the towering peaks. He saw a region to the southwest that looked "promisingly severe". He hoped it might contain the elusive peaks he'd come west to find. His was a casual observation. Looking for something else, he did not comprehend the massive expanse of ice laid out before his very eyes. On his third attempt in 1893, he found Athabasca Pass but discovered only mountains of a much smaller size.

When Coleman first looked upon these "splendid snowfields and peaks", the Athabasca Glacier was much larger than it is now. Moraines left behind as evidence suggest the summers had been shorter and cooler, and snow had fallen deeply in winter on the icefield that formed the glacier's slowly moving tongue. The first descriptions have the Athabasca Glacier extending blue-green and wrinkled over most of the valley. The first visitors could not pass this way without ropes and ice axes. The standard horse route to Jasper passed east of the glacier, over a barren pass named for Walter Wilcox who visited the area in 1896. He, too, had hoped to solve the mystery of David Douglas's giant peaks. Though the Icefields were attracting a lot of attention, the region was still very remote. Climbers and adventurous horsemen were the only ones to encounter the huge ice mass for decades after it was discovered. Travel in this area was difficult until the turn of the century. Huge tracts of forest had been set alight and allowed to burn during construction of the railway. The valley floors were wet, and mosquitoes rose in swarms from the swamps. It often took five weeks for parties to make their way through the tangled forests from the railhead at Lake Louise to the Columbia Icefield. It must have been a stunning experience. Since the highway was officially opened along this route on June 15, 1940, it has been acclaimed as one of the most beautiful drives in the world.

The Giants Are Not Giant At All

The peaks in the Columbia Icefield area are among the highest along the Great Divide, the watershed spine that serves as boundary between the provinces of Alberta and British Columbia. It is the height and dizzying relief of these mountains that first brought the Rockies to the attention of early American and British climbers. Professor Coleman wrote and lectured extensively about these mountains when he returned to Toronto. American and British alpine clubs raced one another for first ascents of the virgin Icefield peaks.

The snow covered peak of Mt. Athabasca, on the left of the panorama, commands a fine view of the Athabasca and Dome Glaciers. The summit also affords excellent views of the Saskatchewan Glacier, a valley glacier similar to the Athabasca, but nearly twice as long. It also provides an excellent vantage to observe the major peaks for miles in every direction. Norman Collie, a British chemistry professor, was the first to climb this mountain. He, too, was in the Rockies searching for David Douglas's Hooker and Brown. It was August 18, 1898 when Collie and Herman Woolley reached the summit. At 3491 metres, over 11,000 feet, this was the highest mountain yet climbed in the Icefield region. From its summit, he saw the extent of the Icefield which gave birth to more than twenty alpine glaciers. Collie also saw and named the mind-slowing bulk of Mt. Columbia and the extreme walls of colossal Mt. Alberta. He saw and named the North and South Twins, distant Mt. Bryce, Snow Dome, and Stutfield Peak. They were grand and beautiful mountains, but they were not the ones for which he searched.

Back at the University of London in England, Collie studied David Douglas's original journals and announced to the climbing world that the exaggerated heights of Mounts Hooker and Brown were based on an error in calculating the altitude of Athabasca Pass. The summit of this long unused trading route was only half the height Douglas had thought. The peaks that surrounded it were barely 9,000 feet high. The giants were not giants at all. This, however, did not reduce the zeal climbers felt for the Icefield and the truly challenging peaks that sprouted from its timeless snows. The alpine olympics had just begun.

Thirty Peaks In Sixty Days

James Outram was the eldest son of a British baronet. Ten years of service to the cloth as a vicar in the Church of England made him an excellent candidate for a nervous breakdown, which he had, then promptly retired from his profession. In 1900 he came to the Rockies to recover his health. The following year, in uttermost secrecy, Outram mounted an expedition to Mt. Assiniboine, the Matterhorn of the Rockies. He scooped the prize right out of the hands of Walter Wilcox who, on a previous attempt, had been repulsed near the summit by bad weather. By 1902, Outram was back. In one season Outram made ten first ascents of peaks over 3050 metres and surveyed four new passes in the Icefield area. His crowning achievement was the twenty-two hour climb of Mt. Columbia. Outram and Swiss guide Christian Kaufmann also climbed Mt. Bryce and Mt. Lyell that year, before joining forces with Norman Collie in successful attempts on Mt. Forbes and Mt. Freshfield.

Outram's feats of endurance and skill were not repeated for two decades. The Rockies were still hard to get to and hard to get through. A world war intervened. It wasn't until 1923, with the arrival of J. Monroe Thorington, a wealthy Philadelphia physician, that climbing really became exciting again. In late June and July of that year, Thorington, W. S. Ladd, and the dean of Swiss guides, Conrad Kain, set something of a new endurance record for Canadian climbing. Driven by sheer exuberance, they climbed the North Twin, Mount Saskatchewan, and Mount Columbia in five days. This does not seem so remarkable until you calculate the height of these mountains and the distances between them. The Thorington party hiked 123 kilometres, nearly 70 miles. Two of these climbs were first ascents, and the total vertical of the three mountains is more than six miles. Stacked on end, they would reach ten kilometres into the sky. It was an amazing five day performance.

This feat was rivalled, however, the next year by an American expedition led by W. O. Field. His group, assisted by the legendary guide Edward Feuz, climbed both the North and South Twins in just over twenty-four hours, a combined distance of fifty-eight kilometres. A mania appeared to be developing. Climbers seemed to relish the ordeal. Though it is difficult to imagine much fun in racing up dangerous mountains, this seemed to be the rage of the day. In 1927, one A. J. Ostheimer and two fellow Harvard students put a new route up the North Twin, made first ascents of Mt. Stutfield and Mt. Kitchener, and made the first traverse of Snow Dome all in only thirty-six hours. During their sixty-three days in the Rockies, they logged over a thousand kilometres and climbed thirty peaks. Twenty-five of these were first ascents.

Tracks Across The Endless Snow

As late as 1930, the travel season in the high Rockies had been confined to late June until the middle of September. Winters were considered inhospitable, and it was too difficult to supply outlying areas in spring until the soft snow had melted from the valleys. Early Swiss guides and Scandinavian immigrants to the region had never looked upon snow as an obstacle, and their enthusiasm soon spread to local residents of Banff and Jasper.

In March of 1932, Cliff White, Joe Weiss, and Russell Bennett skied from Jasper to Banff, a distance, at that time, of 480 kilometres, nearly 300 miles. In the Columbia Icefield area, they made what for years remained the longest run in the history of Canadian skiing. Climbing to the top of Snow Dome, they turned downhill for a distance of fifty kilometres in a total descent of almost three thousand metres. Though vertical descent of these proportions is not uncommon now, it was an exciting development then, focusing plenty of attention on the ski potential of the Rockies.

Winter mountaineering in the Icefield area was not born with one long ski run down Snow Dome. Even Cliff White and his friends knew the limitations of their equipment and the vagaries of the indifferent climate above treeline. Most climbers of the period were happy to leave the winter Rockies to the cold winds and the heavy snows of the annual ice age. Winter climbing was, quite simply, no fun. It was only out of urgent necessity that men started challenging the winter peaks of the Icefield group.

Dwarfed By A Monstrous Tension

World War II was not like any other war. This war would be fought outside the trenches and confined frontiers of international boundaries. It would be fought everywhere, even in mountains. The British Army recognized this early, and in 1943 officers were being trained in the Icefield area as instructors in mountain warfare. In January of 1944, eight hundred Lovat Scouts and two hundred Canadian soldiers trained in Jasper National Park. It was a brutal program. The high degree of training these soldiers experienced can be appreciated in terms of their contribution to the history of Canadian mountaineering. In 1944, troops training at the Icefield made the first winter ascents of Mounts Columbia, Kitchener, Andromeda, and Nigel Peak. Unfortunately, few, if any, would apply their knowledge. The Lovat unit was involved in the early stages of the invasion of Italy. Most of the Scouts did not survive to fight in mountains.

When the war ended, an increasingly affluent public took private cars and longer trips into the mountains. The already completed Banff-Jasper Highway was gaining recognition as the most scenic and accessible part of the Rockies. Bungalow camps, stores, and restaurants were sprouting up all along the route. The first "animal jams" were creating themselves around roadside bears and browsing deer. The most popular attraction along this route, however, was where the road met the snout of a retreating glacier. The Athabasca Glacier, hissing and rumbling with melt, was one place every visitor could go to feel the raw power behind the changing nature of the earth. One could stand speechless and uncomprehending before such obvious power, and it made one feel very small. This mind-slowing scale of the peaks and the ice is still a very confronting part of every visit to the glacier. You feel dwarfed by a monstrous tension, as if the muscles of the trembling earth were about to flex, with you between them.

Mt. Andromeda (3450 m)

ATHABASCA GLACIER 11:05

When I arrived at the Icefield, all operations were closed due to heavy cloud and snow. I made arrangements to go out onto the ice while the weather was opening slightly. The sky opened every few minutes and then would quickly close in blowing snow, hail and rain. The snowcoaches started trips as the weather continued, I quickly set up to capture the scene as the sky opened.

Nigel Peak (3211 m)

Mt. Wilcox (2884 m)

Snow Dome (3451 m)

Athabasca Glacier

THE ATHABASCA GLACIER

A SNOWCOACH ON GLACIER ICE

The Space Age Meets The Ice Age

The idea of a snowcoach concession on the gently dipping snout of the Athabasca Glacier was born in 1948 when a man named Alex Watt attached a half-track to an aging Brewster bus and drove it onto the ice. The inspiration for this rather unusual attraction had come to Watt by way of the Eighty-seventh Mountain Division of the American Army which had performed maneuvers in the Icefield area in 1942. In that year forty-five American soldiers per-formed their own experiments with vehicular transport across the ice. Stationed at the foot of the Saskatchewan Glacier, they drove a variety of jeeps, trucks, half-tracks, and snowmobiles up and down the ice, develop-ing new techniques for road building and crevasse bridging that might prove useful in northern warfare. So successful were these men that they reported actually getting a vehicle to the top of the Snow Dome and landing a Norseman aircraft on the Icefield itself.

The Columbia Icefield snowcoach concession has changed hands, and shape, a great deal since 1948. Originally a small operation capable of carrying a handful of people out onto the ice each day, it has grown into one of the most popular visitor destinations in the Rockies. Now operated by Brewster Transportation and Tours Ltd., the snowcoaches take as many as three thousand passengers a day for a forty-five minute inspection of the glacier's surface. Over the course of a summer, the ride attracts more than a quarter of a million visitors from all over the world. Huge, diesel powered snow machines, built especially for this purpose, carry up to fifty-four people at a time along a carefully located and graded course, while driver/guides point out features of the glacier and explain the dynamics of the Icefield that forms it. The machines look like science-fiction transports designed for use on the surface of another planet. They grind slowly around surficial rivers and great crevasses that open up regularly in the surface of the ice. The passengers, warm and comfortable inside, step out onto the glacier at the end of the snow road and are confronted by the indifference and cold, typical of any ice age landscape. The tour is enormously popular, largely because it is virtually impossible for the average visitor to travel across ice of this depth and magnitude without mountaineering experience and plenty of complicated climbing equipment. The experience is particularly interesting in bad weather, when visitors can witness first-hand the range of climatic influences that have made the Rockies as ruggedly beautiful as they are today.

The Naked Stare Of Space Itself

Though the snowcoach tour is a fine attraction, the best way to fully appreciate the magnitude of the Icefield landscape is to simply stand in the valley alone with it. Visitors tend to be uneasy beneath mountains whose summits are an incomprehensible distance above them. They are uncomfortable in the presence of so much ice. There is a tendency to cluster with others at the snout, or to crowd into the snowcoach ticket line for help in dealing with the uncertainty and humbleness such landscapes induce. There is a mind-stretching airiness in this moonscape. It feels as if the whole valley were purposely carved into a parabola, beaming human insignificance out to the stars. The place is immersed in a strange, busy silence, reminiscent of the Om; the one word of which Buddhists believe the world was formed. It is the sound of the spheres humming, the music around whose notes life has organized itself. People get out of their vehicles to stand in the wind spilling down from the snowfield above. They take one look, feel the knife of the space-cold, and plunge back into their heated cars. But it is not the cold that is confronting. It is the sheer, alien inhospitality of the place. Humans do not belong in this cold. But the wind knows strange tales of our past. It tells the very history of the planet; of its hot beginning, its terrible internal tensions, and the deep bitter cold of its often polar surface. Yes, we know this cold. We were nurtured in it, crossing the windy wastelands of the last age of ice. There is a deep memory of this in all of us. If we are drawn to these places it is because, standing beneath these peaks, there is a vague sense of having been here before. It is like returning to a long forgotten home.

Once inured to the suddenly changing and often bitter weather of the Icefield area, one begins to see a strange and haunting beauty in the features the cold leaves behind. There is the glacier itself. It is white where last winter's snow covers the rock-littered, glass-sharp surfaces of the ice. Where the glacier is contorted as it flows over irregularities, there are gaping blue and green-throated crevasses often rumbling with melt that falls in streams from above. The light on the ice is pure and bright. One sees with a rare clarity often obscured by the crowded places and hectic lives we normally live. Sunlight careens from the high walls of crumbling ice that appear where the glacier stretches and breaks over great cliffs in the bedrock beneath. It bounces sunbright from stairs of blue ice descending the cathedral crags of Mount Andromeda and Snow Dome. It reflects blindingly from the chrome-sparkle of the icefall; the sky an unnerving blue above. Boundaries such as these are mentally confronting; a mystifying numbness pervades that has little to do with the cold. This is the edge, the upward limit of the inhabitable earth. Above, only permanent ice, cold stone, and the naked stare of space itself.

Because of the accessibility of this glacier there has been much scientific study of its dynamics. The areas of research at the Icefield since 1945 include surveys of life in post-glacial environments, the effects of gravity on moving ice, sediment transport on and below the surface of valley glaciers, and radar analysis of depth and shrinkage patterns of glaciers in retreat.

The valleys adjacent to big glaciers are always colder than nearby valleys absent of ice. The Columbia Icefield is so big that warm westerly winds from the Pacific are dramatically cooled as they pass over it. Even on the warmest days, cold breezes sweep down the glacier from the three hundred square kilometres of ice and snow above. But the summers, at least for now, have the upper hand. The glaciers are receding. By their very definition they are in constant advance, but now they are melting faster than they are moving ahead. Though it varies greatly, the glacier's forward movement is about five car lengths a year. Melt, however, erodes the ice at nearly double that rate, causing the glacier to shrink about thirteen metres every summer. Still, its statistics are impressive. The glacier is six and one half kilometres long, roughly forty-five city blocks of grinding, crumbling ice. Its maximum thickness is roughy 300 metres. You could stand the largest man-made building inside it and only see its top. Its density is more than thirteen times that of freshly fallen snow. The glacial mass alone is thought to weigh about 51 billion kilograms, about the weight of one-quarter of the earth's total population. Still, it is a relatively light object compared to the huge mass of stone that surrounds it.

Every geography student has heard of the almost supernatural powers of abrasion attributed to moving ice. Unfortunately, unless you've seen a glacier on the move, you are required to accept the testimonies of geologists on faith. A visit to the Athabasca Glacier, however, can make an ardent sedimentarian out of even the most disinterested bystander. Visitors as wary as those from Missouri will marvel at the amount of debris discharged into the small tarn at the snout of the melting ice. On a warm day, the melt will release as much as five hundred tons of rock flour and gravel into the gray-brown pool called Sunwapta Lake. If this were to continue, and the ice were to melt back and up into the peaks, the resulting scene might resemble modern-day Lake Louise. But the valley here is narrow, and lakes are impermanent marks upon the land. Merely bulges in fast departing rivers, they last only as long as it takes for the water to find a new and faster way to the sea. No lake will form here for long; visitors can continue to marvel at Lake Louise, for it is unique in this land of endless ice and snow.

Visitor reaction to the glacier varies widely. Some are profoundly confronted by the way the land stands on end in the Icefield area. Of these, some feel a claustrophobia from which they cannot escape until, at last, they find themselves again on the open prairies. However, most of the quarter-million annual visitors agree that the first view of the ice is one of the grandest moments in their Canadian Rockies experience. Overcome by heady notions of the great mountaineering traditions, they step boldly onto the snout and climb confidently up the glass crumble of the exposed ice. Their ardour, however, stalls suddenly when, exhausted from the brief but invigorating ascent, they recognize their running shoes or sandals will not hold going down the ice. Yawning crevasses block the way up the glacier and intrepid amateurs are faced with a dangerous slide down the toe, or shouting humilating requests for help from the crowd assembled below. Even very experienced people get into trouble on this glacier. Since the national parks began recording climbing casualties in the Rockies, more than fifty years ago, an average of one person has died on the Athabasca Glacier every year. There is only one area of the Athabasca that one can confidently say is safe from hidden crevasses, rotting snow bridges, and the danger of descent down the sharp ice of the surface. A major effect is made to ensure the safety of this particular route. This is the road the snowcoaches take to the turn-around point beneath the spectacular icefall at the headwall.

The glaciers themselves are not the only hazardous elements of the Icefield terrain. The high meadows that pour down to treeline from the major peaks of the area are outstanding habitat for grizzly bears. One of these meadow systems is hazardous in its own right, even when there are no bears in the area. The Castleguard Meadows, a broad alpine plateau most easily accessible by crossing the lower reaches of the Saskatchewan Glacier, is pock marked with deep pits resembling collapsed mine shafts. The traveller comes upon these holes unexpectedly and peers down into ancient limestone through which water percolates into the longest and, in many ways, most unique cave system in all of Canada.

The Castleguard Cave was first described by the 1924 W. O. Field Expedition during a break in their marathon climbing adventures in the Icefield area. The men were startled by subterranean thunder which, when investigated, proved to be a river issuing forth from a great rent in the side of a mountain. When the flow mysteriously ceased two days later, members of the expedition penetrated the cave to a distance of some two hundred metres. Their way blocked at this point by a deep well, the men exited, relieved to continue their explorations out in the bright mountain light. Though the cave mouth was visited often over the next few decades, no further exploration of the cave was undertaken until the 1960s. By then caving techniques and equipment had evolved enough for full-scale expeditions to tackle the unpredictable caverns. In 1967 the first expedition to the caves in forty-three years found its way to the bottom of the first well. Two members of the expedition were in the cave for eighteen hours when they found their retreat blocked by one of the floods that often fills the cave. In five hours it subsided barely enough for the cavers to escape. Then it rose again and the cave filled with water for the next eighteen days. A 1980 expedition spent ten days exploring the stunning inside scenery of the cave system but was unable to follow all possible leads. Eighteen kilometres of tunnels and passageways were explored. They also found passageways they hadn't time to follow. One channel of the system appeared to end under the Icefield itself, but the true extent of this immense cave system is still a mystery.

That such an extensive cave system should exist around and beneath the Columbia Icefield is not surprising. It serves further notice of the power of ice to utterly alter the nature of the landscapes it occupies. The main névé, or collecting basin where most of the snow still accumulates to form glacial ice, was one of the main cradles out of which the last ice age marched eastward and westward from the spine of the Rockies. When the climate of North America warmed and the ice began to melt fifteen thousand years ago, the volume of water must have been unimaginable compared even to the great torrents of summer melt visitors experience today. Tearing through soft limestone, the water accentuated passageways, which opened into grottos and subway-shaped tubes fashioned in the rock 350,000 years before. But this is the way of water: dissolving, wearing. This is the way of ice: grinding, tearing. Standing on the Athabasca Glacier, one is not just in touch with the ice. One is witness to the very heartbeat of a planet whose days are measured out by a metronome of rising and falling mountains, advancing and retreating glaciers, and evolving and declining life forms. Any notion of permanence falters when, in the cold wind, the rivers carry the mountains away in front of your very eyes.

Mt. Edith Cavell (3363 m)

MOUNT EDITH CAVELL   06:12

The steep face of this peak receives light only at sunrise. To capture this scene requires the use of a split filter. These work best when cut on location to suit each scene. In brief, the filter allows the top one-third of this scene to record as calculated with a meter and the bottom two-thirds will record with twice the exposure. The result is a scene with visible detail in very dark areas.

Throne Mtn. (3120 m)

Cavell Lake

MOUNT EDITH CAVELL

Montagne de la Grande Traverse

Mt. Edith Cavell is by far the most conspicious mountain in the lower Athabasca River Valley. Taller even than the big pyramid that towers over the town of Jasper, Mt. Edith Cavell has long stood as a major landmark for travellers bound for the Great Divide. Before being named for a British nurse in 1916, it was known as La Montagne de la Grande Traverse, for it was in the shadow of its immense peak that early voyageurs tramped toward the Whirlpool River and Athabasca Pass, the first major trading route through the Rocky Mountains.

This route through the Rockies, which became a veritable national highway during the heyday of the fur trade, was discovered by David Thompson in January of 1811. Thompson is North America's premier explorer and cartographer. In his more than thirty years of exploration, he mapped over one and one-half million square miles of wilderness. His great map was so accurate that parts of it were still used a century later. Thompson's narrative of his exploration in the regions now encompassed by Banff and Jasper National Parks is a Canadian classic. It, more than any other document, depicts the brutal conditions in which most of mountainous western Canada was explored and mapped. It offers the reader a vivid sense of what it was like to be completely alone and utterly lost in a hostile land. Only space travel could duplicate this extreme alien feeling today.

David Thompson began his apprenticeship with the Hudson's Bay Company in 1784, at a time when it was in fierce competition with the Northwest Company for fur trade supremacy in the Canadian west. In 1787 Thompson and five men were sent into the most hostile of Indian terrain to persuade the natives to engage in fur trade negotiations with the Hudson's Bay Company. He ran smack into the warlike Piegan Indians, and into the wall of the Rockies. Through careful diplomacy Thompson was able to befriend the Indians, but was unable to make any further progress west. The journey impressed him, however, and gave rise to a fervent desire for further exploration in this new land. In 1797 he joined the competition with the proviso he would be given greater freedom to explore the Rockies. By the turn of the nineteenth century, both companies had established posts right up against the mountains. Strategic advantage could only be gained by the company that was able to find a way through the main ranges of the Rockies, and into the fur-rich interior of what is now British Columbia.

In 1800 at Rocky Mountain House, David Thompson met a ragged band of Kootenay Indians who had crossed the Rockies by an unknown pass to trade. It would have been expedient to join the band on its return trip to learn the route they had taken into the western drainage of the divide. Unfortunately, the Piegan Indians, long time enemies of the Kootenays, were not amused by Thompson's obvious plan. The Piegans had driven the Kootenays across the mountains with guns they got from traders. They preferred the Kootenays to stay permanently on the west side of the divide, unarmed. They made it clear they would be just as happy to solve the problem by killing the thirty-three members of the Kootenay band, whom they outnumbered nearly twenty to one. Thompson, recognizing his own precarious situation, chose to send two of his men to winter with the departing Kootenays, while he continued diplomatic parlay with the local warriors. He and Duncan McGillivary rode south along the mountains with the Piegans to the present site of Calgary.

They asked if the Piegans might help them find a pass. The Piegans issued warnings about the belligerent nature of tribes they might meet and, in the end, offered no assistance to the plan.

In 1806 Thompson was back at Rocky Mountain House where he met more Kootenays who had crossed the Divide. His assistant, Jaco Finlay, went with the departing band to a point where the waters started flowing west. In May of the following year, Thompson was ready to cross the pass. The Piegans, he could tell, were going to block his way. It happened, however, that a courier arrived to tell the Indians that two of their confederates had been killed by the Lewis and Clark Expedition the year before. The Piegans departed for the south, and revenge. Thompson crossed the Great Divide over what is now called Howse Pass, proving conclusively that the Rockies need not block commerce west.

The Kootenays eventually got guns and defeated the Piegans in battle. The

Piegans subsequently blocked the pass for good, making it too dangerous to use the route for trade. Only by finding a way to the Columbia, the great waterway to the Pacific coast, would the west be opened up. So great was the urgency that an expedition was mounted at the outset of the Canadian winter. On October 28, 1810, Thompson left Rocky Mountain House for the Athabasca River. In thirty-eight days his party reached Brule Lake, near what is now Jasper Park. They were starving and it was bitterly cold. They made a crude camp and stayed a month to recuperate. In January of 1811, they proceeded west. In deep snow and under heavy loads they passed La Montagne de la Grande Traverse and started up the Whirlpool River to Athabasca Pass. When they reached it, they were in poor shape. It was brutal country and Thompson's men had had enough. From Thompson's journal:

"The view before us was an ascent to deep snow, in all appearance ... the height of land between the Atlantic and Pacific Oceans; it was to me an exhilarating sight, but to my uneducated men the scene of desolation before us was dreadful ... Many reflections came on my mind; a new world was in a manner before me, and my object was to be at the Pacific Ocean before the month of August, but how were we to find provisions, and how many men would remain with me ... ?"

Distance and desolation were not Thompson's only enemies. Myths brought west with his men made everyone nervous. This was unknown country. No one knew what creatures occupied it. Other expeditions had discovered bones of huge beasts. Thompson's men thought these mountains were haunted:

"Strange to say here is the strong belief that the haunt of the mammoth is about this defile. None can positively say that they had seen him, but their belief I found firm and not to be shaken. I remarked to them that such an enormous animal must leave indelible marks of his feet and his feeding. This they all acknowledged (but) all I could say did not shake their belief in his existence."

For the next fifty years, wanderers travelled over Athabasca Pass en route to the Pacific. It was a route for fur traders and the occasional adventurer. This was not a land that invited one to linger and, at best, the Rockies were considered an inconvenient barrier that had to be crossed. The prevalent attitude of travellers in this period is portrayed in the journals of Ross Cox who crossed the pass in 1817, "I'll take my oath, my dear friends, that God Almighty never made such a place!"

Modern travellers might wonder why early explorers and fur traders found it difficult to celebrate the stunning beauty that it is obvious in this landscape. In fact, the journals of early travellers do describe a certain mood of awe for what they saw. This, however, is overshadowed by the danger and privation that were always part of the experience in this remote land. Though the Indians were not the only hazard, they were considered a formidable one. It was a well established fact that, if you wanted to survive in the west, you had to get along carefully with the natives. Before crossing Athabasca Pass, Ross Cox worked with the Astoria Company in what is now Montana. On Christmas Day, 1812, he witnessed a spectacle that typified the violence warring tribes could bring upon one another and, ostensibly, upon belligerent whites. The Flathead Indians were torturing a Blackfoot they had captured in battle.

"The Flatheads had gathered around a fire to witness the spectacle. Some of them heated an old gun barrel until it turned red and then burnt stripes as if to make a pattern on the legs, the thighs, the cheeks and the neck of the prisoner, who stood perfectly motionless against a tree to which he was tied. They then cut the flesh about his nails and separated his finger joints one by one.

The Blackfoot never winced. Instead he laughed and goaded them on to further efforts. "My heart is strong", he would say, "you cannot hurt me, you are like fools. Try it again, you don't know how to do it. We torture your relatives far better, because we make them cry aloud like children." A Flathead who had lost one eye in an encounter years before, was standing sullenly near the fire. So the prisoner taunted him. "It was by my arrow that you lost your eye. Do you remember?" Thereupon the one-eyed brave darted at him and gouged one of his eyes from his socket for revenge. Undisturbed the Blackfoot now looked with his remaining eye at another of his tormentors and said, "It was I who killed your brother and scalped your father. Have you so soon forgotten?" At this provocation the Flathead warrior sprung up like a panther, scalped his insulter and would have plunged a knife into his heart had he not been advised to desist. It was now the turn of the head-chief to be insulted by the bleeding prisoner at the stake. "It was I that made your wife a slave last year. We put out her eyes, tore out her tongue and treated her like a dog." A shriek of rage greeted these words. The chief seized his gun and before the sentence was complete shot a ball through the prisoners heart, thus ending his frightful ordeal."

It was patently clear you didn't mess with the Indians.

Though not quite as horrifying, the journals of Gabriel Franchère are filled with further harrowing tales. In 1810 Franchère sailed from New York aboard the Tonquin, a trading ship owned by John Jacob Astor, an American fur trade giant. By March of the following year, the Tonquin was nearing the mouth of the Columbia River where the men hoped to build a fort and control the large trading area the river served. Under the tyrannical command of Captain Thorn, five men were dispatched in small boats and high seas to explore the shoreline. They never returned. The Captain got his due, however. While Fort Astoria was being constructed, the Captain sailed north along the coast to trade with the Indians. An altercation developed and the arrogant Thorn and his unfortunate crew were murdered. Back at Fort Astoria the men faced further problems. The War of 1812 complicated boundary issues in what was still British Territory. The Northwest Company announced to the Astorians that a British naval blockade would prevent Astor's company from supplying the fort. Realizing the bleakness of the situation, the Astorians sold the fort to the Northwest Company. The new owner offered Astor's men positions with the company or transportation east. His dreams of riches dashed, Franchère chose the long trip home over Athabasca Pass.

In the half century that Athabasca Pass was a prominent trans-continental route, it was travelled by a wide range of men and women in search of wealth and adventure. Many of them went back to England or Europe and wrote about the hardships and, to an ever increasing extent, about the beauty and wildness of the Canadian west. These adventure books were gobbled up by a society that took its colonialism seriously. One of the most important of these books was written by the Scottish botanist, David Douglas, sent to collect specimens by the Horticultural Society of London. In April of 1827, he crossed Athabasca Pass from the Columbia, laden with forty pounds of botanical samples, including cones from the fir tree which would eventually carry his name. Like many visitors of the time, he was mightily impressed with what he saw at the pass. "No matter how familiar one had become with high snowy mountains," he said, "all that we had seen before was forgotten before these high, indescribably sharp and rugged peaks, glaciers and snow." In an earlier map, Douglas had read that the summit of Athabasca Pass was at an altitude of over 10,000 feet.

From this he calculated the summits of the surrounding mountains, which he named Mt. Hooker and Mt. Brown, to be between 16,000 and 18,000 feet. Out of sheer desire he climbed one of these, to become the first man to ascend a peak on the continental divide of North America. His miscalculations of the summits of these two mountains initiated a controversy that, seventy five years later, brought climbers to the Rockies. Douglas continued his work, although his eyesight was failing, until, in Hawaii, he fell into an occupied animal trap and was gored to death by a bull.

The forests below La Montagne de la Grande Traverse are still silent, just as they were in Thompson's time and when David Douglas passed east on his way home to England and lasting fame. Those who followed in their footsteps built trails and roads. Soon the trains came bearing a new generation of adventurers and romantics whose passion for wildness led to the preservation of these vast tracts as national parks. Still, the old trails are there, and sometimes at abandoned camps, hikers find musket balls and trade beads around the buried ashes of fires long dead. Few places remain the same, and for this reason scenes of grand and ageless panorama become meccas for those who wish to measure their lives against a stolid backdrop of frozen time. It is an odd juxtaposition of realities. There is no hurry, the wind says; the peaks remain indifferent. But, it is we who are confined by time. A short life is a poor response to a mountain. There are only so many passes we have time to explore.

onder Peak (2852 m)

Mt. Cautley (2880 m)

Mt. Assiniboine Lodge

Mt. Magog (3095 m)

Mt. Assiniboine (3618 m)

Lake Magog

MOUNT ASSINIBOINE   07:40

This is a very difficult peak to photograph. The steep face is visible in this valley only in the very early morning light. The sun was at a low angle and is hidden behind the bell tower on the lodge. This strong light skims the surface of the snow in the foreground, leaving catchlights. The mountain often creates its own weather and is rarely seen without clouds hanging from the summit.

Sunburst Peak (2820 m)

Wedgewood Peak (2940 m)

t. Terrapin (2944 m)

The Towers (2846 m)

Wonder Pass (2425 m)

MOUNT ASSINIBOINE

THE MATTERHORN OF THE ROCKIES

Wind-shaped Into An Arrow Point

On a clear day, from a high pass or ridge, one can see Mt. Assiniboine from one hundred kilometres away. It stands sharply and easily recognizable above all the peaks in the southern Rockies. Its remoteness, sheer size, and imposing steepness have made it a place to where hikers and climbers have made pilgrimages since white men first made their way into these mountains. Even today, a visitor to the Rockies is not considered serious, within devout mountaineering circles, unless he or she has undertaken a visit to this mountain.

This deceptive panorama was taken from Assiniboine Lodge as the winter sun brightened toward spring and the March snows were at their best for skiing. Mt. Assiniboine itself, distantly out of perspective at the centre of the group of large mountains forming its massif, forms part of the border between Mt. Assiniboine Provincial Park and Banff National Park. At 3618 metres, it is the highest peak in both parks.

Archaeological evidence indicates the first people to visit and frequent the mountain were the Kootenay Indians who lived on the west side of the continental divide. Although there is no proof natives lived year round near this particular mountain, they saw it regularly as they made their way across passes connecting them to other Indian traders on the plains. Because it was a difficult mountain to miss, early explorers, even if they didn't visit it, noted the windy pyramid. Later visitors remarked on the similarity between its imposing bulk and the shape of the Matterhorn of the Alps.

The first man to record seeing the mountain was Father De Smet who crossed White Man's Pass in 1845. On his primitive map he marked a big pyramid which, in all likelihood, was the great mountain he would have been able to see from the summit. In 1884 George Dawson, the humpbacked eccentric who headed the Geological Survey of Canada, was working in the eastern part of the Rockies. He recorded seeing the glistening wedge from the summit of Copper Mountain near Banff. In 1885 it was he who gave the mountain its present name. He named it for the Stoney Indians, a race of the plains Sioux who migrated into the eastern Rockies once they became horsemen. It was a practice of this tribe to boil their food, including meat. They did this by dropping hot rocks into water-filled skin bags sunken into hollows in the earth. The people were originally called "Stone-Boilers", but this name was shortened to "Stoney". Their own name for their tribe, however, was "Assiniboine".

The first recorded expedition that actually went to the mountain was led by Tom Wilson, the famous Banff guide and outfitter credited with discovering both Lake Louise and Emerald Lake. His client was one Robert L. Barrett, a Chicago paper manufacturer and business magnate, a man with a seemingly mad desire to climb mountains just for sport. In 1893 he and Wilson, with George Fear as cook, rode from the Sunshine area of what is now Banff National park in hopes that Barrett would have an opportunity to attempt the big peak from a camp below the face. The season was late, however, and Barrett never got his chance at the mountain.

Secret Sorties To The High Peak

The first actual attempt to climb Mt. Assiniboine took place in the summer of 1899. The expedition was ostensibly led by Walter Wilcox and included Henry Bryant and Louis Steele. They left Banff on July 22 with horses and a complete outfit, but no climbing guide. They took a route proposed by Tom Wilson that followed Healy Creek to the Sunshine area and over Citadel Pass. Beleaguered by a snow storm, they camped below Mt. Assiniboine at a site Wilcox recognized from his first visit to the mountain in 1895. While Wilcox went back to retrieve a rucksack fallen from one of the horses, Bryant and Steele tried to scale the mountain. In 1899 the glacier that pours down the north side of the mountain was much larger than it is today. Reaching almost all the way to Lake Magog, the two climbers used this route to gain access to the snowfield above. Though the snow conditions made progress slow, the two reached three thousand metres on the mountain before they were forced back by the advance of yet another storm. Despite a minor accident on the descent, the two made it safely back to the lake where they camped for four days waiting for conditions to improve. During this time Wilcox made many of his famous early pictures of the lake and surrounding views, but no further progress was made toward the summit.

The following year another attempt was made on Assiniboine by two amateur climbers from Chicago. Turned back from the summit by the first vertical cliff bands, the brothers Willoughby and English Walling appear to have made a bit of a mess of the whole affair. Their defeat was made further ignominious when they lost their way on the trip back from the mountain. If anything, their expedition is notable only for the fact that theirs was the first to use Swiss guides on an attempt of Mt. Assiniboine.

It appears that a few failures on a large mountain add immeasurably to that mountain's status in the eyes of the climbing community. Mt. Assiniboine, it appeared, was a real challenge, and the first to climb it would be worthy of laurels and high public praise. It was clear the mountain was not impossible. Quite simply, it would be conquered by the first man to arrive at the mountain in good conditions and with enough supplies to make a prolonged push for the summit. To this end, expeditions became increasingly secretive, and in a very quiet way, a race was on for the peak.

In 1901 Wilcox and Bryant were back again, this time with able Swiss guides. They made a very determined effort to climb the mountain from the southwest side. But the conditions were not right. It was late in the season; snow and rain greeted them as they approached the peak. Though they reached the highest point yet attained on the mountain, the expedition was driven back by avalanches and bitter cold. It was a great disappointment for Wilcox on his last chance at the big mountain before others reached its summit.

Word quickly got out about the latest failed attempt on the Canadian Matterhorn. Wilcox's expedition was discussed in detail among climbers camped in the Rockies that year. It just so happened that 1901 was a big year for Canadian climbing; that summer the CPR brought to the Rockies the "Prince of Mountaineers", Sir Edward Whymper himself. Whymper, after seven attempts, had made the first ascent of the real Matterhorn in 1865. Five years after his ascent, every major European peak had been climbed. Surely, to be consistent with his great accomplishment in the Alps, the great climber would be after the summit prize of Mt. Assiniboine. The CPR had done everything it could to ensure the famous climber a successful season, including cancellation of the topographical survey planned for the Rockies that summer. Whymper brought with him his own highly trained team of Swiss guides. There was no telling what they might do. As fate would have it though, the sixty-two year old Whymper had no intention of risking his fame on a mountain he wasn't sure he could climb. He would leave Assiniboine to a younger man.

James Outram heard about Wilcox's unsuccessful attempt while visiting Yoho with Whymper and decided, though the season was late, he would make just one try for the summit. The famous climber's interest in Assiniboine was no doubt fueled by a promise made by his outfitter, none other than Bill Peyto, that he could lead Outram's expedition to the foot of the mountain in only two days. Peyto also baited Outram with the claim that there would be no chance of failure for an experienced mountaineer. On August 31, 1901, at 1:30 pm, they set out from Banff and, true to his word, Peyto had his party at the base of the mountain on the evening of the next day. On September 2nd, Outram's party tried from the southwest and failed, returning to camp in darkness. The weather was clear the next day and, making use of a cache established in their previous failed attempt, they made for the peak from the south arête. Spending nearly two glorious hours at the summit they descended by the north face, traversing the mountain as they returned to camp. They broke camp the following day and headed slowly to Banff. Another storm struck the mountain and they plodded back through heavy snow. Typically, perhaps, the day they chose to climb was the only "window" the weather permitted to the summit in several days.

The first ascent by a woman took place in 1904 when Gertrude Benham, a famous English mountaineer, made the ascent with two local guides. It is not remarkable that women were capable of climbing such formidable peaks. What is impressive is that they often did so dressed in the attire of the day, which for ladies usually meant long skirts and petticoats below the knee. In the Victorian era, it was a sign of good breeding to be appropriately dressed wherever you were. It was not uncommon for gentlemen to wear tweed jackets and ties as they grunted their way to the summits, and of course ladies were required to dress accordingly, wherever they went.

Wheeler's Walking Tours

Though many other expeditions would come to the mountain to find more challenging and difficult routes, the history of the Assiniboine area in the 1920s is associated with a man whose interest in the Rockies made them accessible to visitors from abroad. Arthur Wheeler was one of the principal surveyors involved in the Interprovincial Boundary Survey that mapped all the mountains along the border of Alberta and British Columbia. In 1906 Wheeler, a consummate mountaineer, helped organize the Alpine Club of Canada and served as its president until 1910. A decade later Wheeler initiated his famous Walking Tours, great loop trips that took enthusiasts on long outings into the very best backcountry in the Rockies. One of his most popular destinations was Assiniboine.

A Terrible Accident

The Walking Tour Camp of 1921 brought to the area an American doctor and his wife who were anxious to climb Mt. Eon, another giant at over three thousand metres, south of Mt. Assiniboine. Their tragic story is one of the most gripping sagas in Canadian climbing. On July 15th of that year, Dr. and Mrs. Winthrop E. Stone set out from Assiniboine Camp with four days of supplies. On the morning of the seventeenth, they made an early start over Mt. Gloria by way of the col and started on a new route on the south face of Mt. Eon. After making excellent progress all day, at about 6:00 pm they encountered a wide, steep chimney with dangerous sloping sides reaching up to the summit. After placing his wife securely at its base and clear of any rockfalls, Dr. Stone ascended until he could see over the slope, but was still unable to see whether a higher point lay beyond. The rest is recorded in the Canadian Alpine Journal of 1922:

"Dr. Stone then climbed out of the chimney and disappeared for a minute or so and shortly afterwards, without any warning, a large slab of rock tumbled off from above, passing over Mrs. Stone, and was closely followed by Dr. Stone, who spoke no word but held his ice axe firmly in his right hand. Horror stricken at the sight, Mrs. Stone braced herself to take the jerk of the rope, not realizing that the Doctor had taken it off in order to explore beyond its length."

Letting herself down another broken chimney to a ledge she thought would lead her to the valley, Margaret Stone found herself ten feet short of rope. She leapt to the ledge only to find that it did not give access to the scree slope below. Unable to build rocks up to the rope hanging useless above her, she was forced to remain without food or shelter until being rescued on Sunday the 24th, eight days after the accident happened.

The Building Of The Lodge

One large and five small cabins, known as the Naiset Cabins, were constructed as part of an arrangement whereby the Alpine Club of Canada purchased land at the foot of Mt. Assiniboine. In 1924 the Alpine Club granted a lease to Wheeler for use of the property and the cabins at two dollars per annum. In 1927 Wheeler sublet the buildings to a half Russian, half Italian nobleman who was Winter Sports Director of the Lake Placid Company in New York. All accounts suggest that Marquis Nicholas degli Albizzi was a genuine character. Certainly, few can question his impact on the Assiniboine area.

In the spring of 1928, Albizzi and his friend Erling Strom, who taught skiing at Lake Placid, planned a winter visit to the Assiniboine area. Local outfitters and guides thought the expedition a little impractical and discouraged them from such madness. Undeterred, however, the duo made their difficult way through the downed timber of burned-out valleys to the safety of the cabins at Assiniboine. The weather broke after they arrived and they enjoyed seventeen days of outstanding skiing. So enthusiastic was Albizzi about the potential of the great peak as a visitor attraction, that he approached the CPR on the possibility of building a major lodge in the meadows below the mountain. It opened in 1929, but not without problems. The Marquis quickly grew disillusioned with the place and it fell into the hands of outfitter Bill Brewster who ran it only in summer. Erling Strom, returning from a visit to Norway, engaged the use of the lodge in the winter months and gradually assumed responsibility for the buildings all year round. Assiniboine Lodge remained much as the panorama shows. Strom ran it until 1966 when he relinquished management to his daughter, Siri. Erling Strom, who loved the area a great deal, continued to visit the lodge in summers until 1978, the year that marked his fiftieth year in the Rockies. The lodge is now operated by Sepp and Barb Renner who maintain its rustic charm and still grant visitors the same awesome opportunity the first adventurers experienced when they found their way to this remote peak.

Mt. Lyautey (3082 m)

Mt. Sarrail (3174 m)

Opal Range

KANANASKIS VALLEY   09:10

The helicopter barely had room to land on a small ridge
below the surrounding peaks. In fact, only the front portion
of the skids were balanced. As the sun rose over the eastern
range, the air warmed and the valley cloud dispersed to
reveal a clear day. I waited until the shadow moved from the
snow covered lakes below, and then made several exposures.
The helicopter returned, and when the films were processed
I found two of the films had frozen and cracked.

Elk Range

Elk Pass (1984 m)

Kananaskis Valley

Spray Range

Mt. Indefatigable (2670 m)

Lower Kananaskis Lake

Upper Kananaskis Lake

THE KANANASKIS VALLEY

SITE OF THE XV WINTER OLYMPICS

In Possession Of Spirit Powers

The Kananaskis Valley was once part of Banff National Park until corporations with resource interests succeeded in having it redesignated to allow hydro development, logging, and mining in the valley. It now adjoins Banff National park on its southern and eastern boundary, and is preserved by a variety of tenuous regulations that govern public lands serving as recreational playgrounds for the residents of Alberta. Now, after years of resource exploitation, the Kananaskis Valley has emerged as a site of major archaeological importance.

In the 1970s a series of archaeological excavations was undertaken by Dr. Brian Reeves of the University of Calgary to determine how extensively the valley was used by native people in prehistoric times. The archaeological team knew from early documents, such as the Palliser Expedition's papers, that North Kananaskis Pass was a main route the Kootenay Indians used to cross the Rockies to trade at Old Bow Fort in the early 1800s. The sites these archeologists discovered proved much older. The earliest recovered artifacts indicated that prehistoric man had been present in the Kananaskis for at least eight thousand years. Excavations in other parts of the eastern slopes indicate men may have frequented some areas of the Rockies for two thousand years longer than they did the valley of the Kananaskis.

The bulk of the unearthed artifacts came from quarry sites in the valley, where large amounts of waste material from the manufacture of stone tools indicate they were made by a particular native culture called the Mummy Cave Complex. This tradition in stone tool development appears to have dominated the area between 5000 and 7500 years ago. Reeves and his group were able to correlate these materials with those discovered at other sites in southern Alberta, British Columbia, and the northern United States. This information yielded evidence about this people's movements from season to season, and gave testimony as to the hunting techniques they were able to employ.

Modern archaeological evidence has changed our notions about native people's presence in these mountains. Until very recently, anthropologists were suggesting that man didn't live in the Rockies until early native peoples acquired the horse. Now it is clear that, at least in the front ranges, people occupied the lower valleys for a period of nearly ten thousand years. During this period, two major developments took place that are of significance to modern man. Firstly, the climate changed in a dramatic way. Secondly, native people adjusted successfully to that change and prospered. They had a culture and way of life permitting them to respond quickly and survive rapid changes in the environment. The question for us is whether or not we could do the same.

Another significant detail of Indian culture yielded by archaeological research is the extent to which the mountains were regarded as the spiritual home of native people. A courageous warrior or medicine man could be purified and his soul guided through life by powerful spirits if he could experience a vision on a remote mountain known to possess special powers. Such vision quest sites are common along the front ranges of the Rockies, and many are still visited by Indians seeking to redefine themselves through their ancient faith in the spirit world. Little is known about these rites, for most modern Indians either don't acknowledge the significance of the vision quest sites, or they are unwilling to share this knowledge with whites.

The native silence of this valley was not punctuated until 1854, when an expedition led by James Sinclair made its difficult way through the tangled forests to the summit of Kananaskis Pass. Sinclair engaged a Cree Indian chief named Mackipictoon at Edmonton House to guide his large group over the unexplored pass at the head of what the chief called the "Strong Current River". Though lost and in somewhat desperate shape, confused records imply the group and their 250 head of cattle likely crossed what is now known as South Kananaskis Pass by way of Three Isle Creek. Because of steep cliff bands below Three Isle Lake, this remains an arduous hike even with a trail. It is no wonder others didn't use the Sinclair route, and the valley remained silent for decades to come.

The first formal expedition to the area was undertaken by Captain John Palliser in 1858. On assignment with the British government, his expedition was to explore and map the endless barrier of stone that separated the prairies from the Pacific. Palliser claims he named Kananaskis Pass after "an Indian of whom there is a legend, giving an account of his most wonderful recovery from the blow of an axe, which had stunned but failed to kill him." His party explored the Kananaskis ranges and some of the valleys now encompassed by Waterton Lakes, Kootenay, Banff, and Yoho National Parks. His final report also pronounced on the agricultural potential of the area. Palliser concluded that it was a wild, brutal land, and though it was beautiful, it would not support settlers.

The observations of the Palliser Expedition are central to our understanding of the west at the time of early European exploration of the Rockies. John Sullivan, an astronomer and secretary to the expedition, was with Palliser when he first came into contact with the Stoney Indians of the Kananaskis Valley. The Stoneys had only recently migrated into the valley and already they had been influenced by the work of missionaries sent to make hostile country safe for the growing number of settlers moving west. Sullivan recorded the meeting in his journals.

"I had a long talk with the chiefs about what was likely to become of them and the other Indian tribes. They said that every year they find it more difficult to keep from starving, and that even the buffalo cannot be depended upon as before, because being now only in large bands, when one tribe of Indians are hunting then the other tribes have to go without until the band migrates into their country. The Stoneys are all Christians, and some of them can read and write in their own language, using the Cree syllabic characters, which were invented by the Wesleyan missionaries. They are very desirous of having tools and a few simple agricultural implements; and as they are very steady, I have no doubt that if they were supplied with these, and direction given to their efforts, the best part of them would soon settle down, and leave their vagrant mode of life. Their chiefs at least seem to be quite in earnest about the matter."

Sullivan's impression does not inspire an image of the noble savages in grand and intimate contact with the land.

Scars On The Trees, Holes In The Ground

Thirty years after the Palliser Expedition, a railway began to thunder through the Rockies along the Bow River north of the Kananaskis. What hadn't been burned over by lightning fires in the lower valley was divided into timber berths, and the forests were logged to make ties. For decades people came looking for gold. Somehow the Kananaskis became identified with the "Lost Lemon Mine" reputedly located somewhere near the headwaters of the Oldman and Highwood Rivers. The only mineral located in the early years, however, was coal, and the grade was not sufficiently high to cause much excitement. Georgetown, Bankhead,

and Anthracite to the north yielded the hard coal the trains burned; what the Kananaskis had could only be used as coke. For decades people exploited the valley then left, leaving only scars on the trees and gaping holes in the ground. The century would turn before anyone would come to stay.

George Pocaterra was born in Rocchette, Italy into an ancient aristocratic family involved in the manufacture of textiles. Having attended university in Switzerland, he was fluent in four languages. He was attracted to the Canadian west in 1903, and soon he was able to add Stoney to the list of languages he knew. Beginning his Canadian experience in Winnipeg, Pocaterra moved to High River, Alberta in 1905 where he hired on as wrangler with the Bar D Ranch. Soon he and an equally adventurous cousin were homesteading the Buffalo Head Ranch in Eden Valley. In the winter of 1906, he started trapping in the Upper Kananaskis. Establishing a close relationship with the Stoneys, his name became increasingly associated with the valley. Soon he was a blood brother to Paul Amos and a close friend of Three Buffalo Bulls, two prominent Stoneys with whom he shared the adventure of travel through a valley that was soon to change forever by the building of a dam.

Nearby, the city of Calgary began to expand. Westward settlement and the railway made it a strategically located centre, and new electrical technology promised it could continue to grow. The Bow, just east of where it was joined by the Kananaskis River, was chosen for the site of the first dam. The Horseshoe Falls power plant was built in 1911 and became the basis of the power grid that in time would include much of the province. The dam was very successful in supplying early power requirements for the city. The superiority of electricity over other forms of energy was clearly demonstrated, and the demand grew far beyond the generation capacity of the first dam. There was simply not enough water, at least not enough for consistent electrical generation all year round. Soon a plan was put forward to dam the Kananaskis Lakes in order to take full advantage of the water storage capacity of the upper valley. Soon the Kananaskis River itself was considered an acceptable power source. By 1932 a hand-hewn spillway was being built on the Upper Kananaskis Lake. Though it had been recognized as early as 1914 that the Kananaskis Valley had enormous potential as a tourist resort area, power developers of the day did not acknowledge minimum environmental impact concepts as they do today. It was not long before the lakes were changed completely. Meanwhile, Pocaterra had gone to Europe with his new wife, the famous opera singer Norma Piper. When he returned from Italy at the beginning of the Second World War, he found that combined logging, mining, and power developments had changed the valley beyond what he could accept. He was crestfallen at the transformation:

"The most beautiful mountain scenery in the world, as far as I am concerned, was at these lakes but now is completely spoiled by these power dams, the drowning of the marvelously beautiful islands and exquisitely curved beaches, the cutting down of the centuries old trees, and the drying up of the twin falls below the lower lake."

Pocaterra left the valley in disgust.

Postwar North America was flamboyant, and hungry for resources. This was a period of almost uncontrolled use of the valley. If anything, damage to the valley during the twenty years following the war demonstrated the urgent need for careful government legislation for the use of public lands. The valley continued to be logged, mined, hunted, and over-used. People went there, it seems, to torture the countryside with four-wheel drive vehicles, axes, and saws and an almost malicious ignorance that typifies a total disregard for the fragility of natural systems. It became very clear that if the Kananaskis Valley was to survive as an integrated biological system, regulations had to be developed to control use. People had to decide what they wanted the valley to become.

It took until the early 1970s for the people of Alberta to recognize the importance of the eastern slopes of the Rockies. Through a series of public forums, provincial resource planners were able to divide the area into management zones based on appropriate use patterns. Four thousand square kilometres was set aside as Kananaskis Country. Some of the best of the high country in this region was later set aside as Kananaskis Provincial Park and made subject to regulations that would preserve it as a public recreational wilderness. Later, it was renamed in honour of the Premier of Alberta under whose leadership the plan had been implemented.

Peter Lougheed Provincial Park still faces many of the problems inherited at its inception. There are still major power developments within the park. Though the mining and lumber operations have ceased activities in the area, it was not designation of the park that was responsible. There were simply no minerals left to exploit, nor trees to cut in the new park area. Peter Lougheed, himself, put the situation in the best perspective during an interview following his retirement from provincial politics. He aptly described the government's involvement with the Kananaskis Valley:

> "Kananaskis Country is a personal dream of mine that I was involved with as Premier of Alberta. In 1977 it came to fruition because we felt unless it was a controlled area, both in terms of wilderness and recreation, it would be frittered away in a multitude of disjointed uses."

Probably the greatest single achievement of Kananaskis Country and Peter Lougheed Provincial Park is their unparalleled success in rehabilitating the damaged landscapes of the region. In the short few years since the park and the preserve were set aside, the character of the entire valley has changed. New trails, new facilities and a completely altered public attitude toward the valley have made it one of the most popular visitor attractions in the province. In fact, it has become a model of how heavily and badly misused landscapes can be recovered and made useful again. Many visitors now prefer the park to the perhaps more spectacular, but certainly more heavily visited national park that adjoins it. Criticism of the high cost of rehabilitating the valley will certainly fade, as Albertans and their guests bask in the increasing significance of what they have done to save one of the most precious landscapes in the front ranges of the Rocky Mountains.